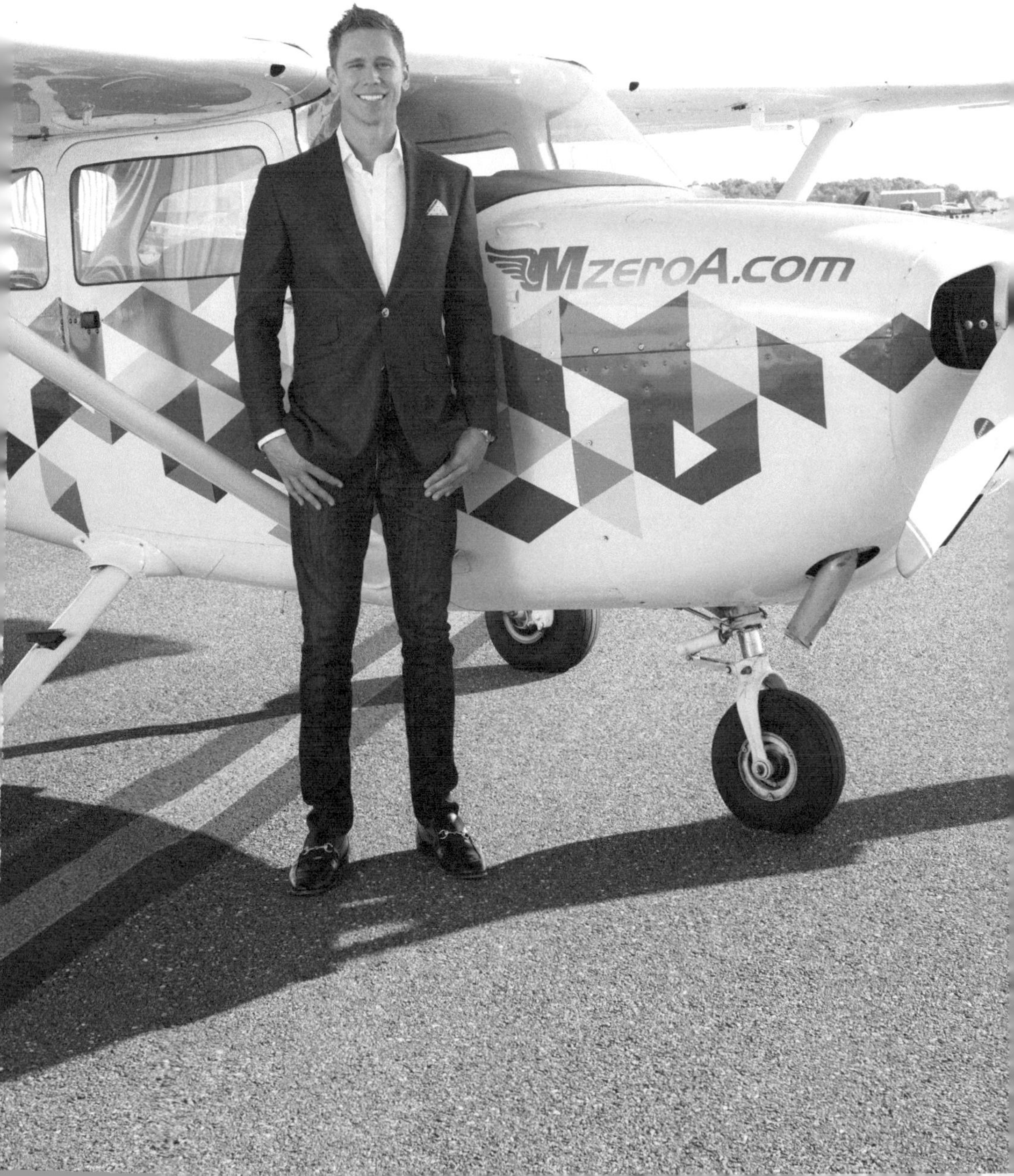

MW01397423

Pass Your Private Pilot Checkride

EDITION 5

Jason Schappert, CFII

MzeroA (pronounced M-zero-A) is an online ground school and flight training community that helps thousands of members per month pass their FAA knowledge tests, checkrides, and helps those members to keep learning after obtaining their certificates and ratings. We believe "A Good Pilot Is Always Learning" is truly a statement to live by. You can learn more about the benefits of our Online Ground School by visiting MzeroA.com.

Copyright © 2024 Jason Schappert, MzeroA
Pass Your Private Pilot Checkride
by Jason Schappert

All rights reserved. No part of this publication may be reproduced, distributed, or transmitted in any form or by any means, including photocopying, recording, or other electronic or mechanical methods, without the express written permission of the publisher, except for the use of brief quotations in critical reviews and other noncommercial uses as permitted by copyright law.

ISBN 10: 8985397055
ISBN 13: 979-8985397055

A Note From The Author

What if we showed up every day to be better versions of ourselves? Gaining more each day — more knowledge, understanding, and real-world skills. This is my reason for this book and MzeroA.com. Everyday we ask: What can we do today to create safer, smarter pilots?

My goal is to keep you inspired in pursuing Aviation Mastery. Mastery in aviation, or any pursuit, has no finish line. This book is filled with motivational messages, the science of learning and aviation safety from my 10,000+ hours as a pilot and flight instructor.

When I started, I never imagined we'd be here today. My dream was to be a military aviator, specifically flying the USAF F15-E. My parents owned a pest control business, and my mom was a nurse. I didn't come from an aviation family, and my grades were poor. My mother loves to share stories of my elementary school report card full of C's and D's, with a note that read: "Jason won't stop talking. He'll talk to anyone. I believe he would talk to the window if it would talk back!" The only perfect grade I received that year was on a final project titled "Pilot," earning a full score, saving my GPA.

At age 12, my father did pest control for a local realtor who offered me a flight lesson in exchange. It was a deal, and I was hooked!

At age 15, we got serious with my lessons. Dad began pressure washing for extra money, and Mom picked up extra shifts. I worked at a paintball field for $40 a day in cash. It all went towards my dream.

Everyone's journey looks different. No matter where you are in your aviation journey, there is more to be done and to learn. Whether you're a prospective student pilot or a rusty pilot, approach this book with a student mindset. We say a good pilot is always learning. It's a statement to live by. Thank you for embarking on this journey towards Aviation Mastery and for making MzeroA one of the best!

Jason Schappert

Praise For The Book

Did you know that this book is available on audible.com? Many learners find it helpful to use this audio version so that they can take the book with them on the road, in the car, in the gym and simply when working around the house.

All the same valuable information can be delivered right to your ears, saving you time and giving you even more opportunity to learn and study throughout the day.

Don't take our word for it, check out these 5 star reviews given by satisfied customers.

Kudos to you and the Mzeroa team!
This past weekend, I passed my PPL checkride.
The Pass your Checkride audio was great. Honestly, I must have listened to the entire book 10+ times over the past 2 months. Driving to work, at the gym, walking the dog, etc. etc. I was definitely overprepared, but had the confidence to answer ANY scenario given to me.
Overprepared...NEVER! A good pilot is always learning.
Time to start IFR.

— Craig Alexander

I just wanted to tell the team at MzeroA that I passed my Private Pilot today. The DPE said "I don't know what you used to study, but I wish all of my check rides were as knowledgeable as you are." 90% of my knowledge came from MzeroA and Pass your Private Pilot Checkride. I'm tired of studying and tired of listening to Jason's voice on audible but couldn't be happier with the outcome.
Thanks again. Hope Jason and all the team gets to know how much I appreciate the program.
Cheers!

— Nickolas Fowler

I'm excited to report that last week I passed my private pilot check ride and earned my temporary airman's certificate. A major contribution to my success came from repeatedly listening to Jason's audio book "Pass your Private Pilot Checkride". The DPE commented that I was one of the best prepared candidates (oral) that he's ever evaluated – not bad for a 61 yo student pilot. That said – Jason's book really helped prepare me.

- **Colin Fagan**

How To Use This Book

This book is unlike anything else on the market. It offers real world checkride questions that not only exceed ACS guidelines but is written from the perspective of a Designated Pilot Examiner.

Use the book to quiz your knowledge. This compact book is full of valuable information and is easy to take with you anywhere you go. Download the audiobook from Audible or the App Store and listen on your commute, while at the gym, or walking down the street. Find ways to immerse yourself in these questions. Make them part of your thought process.

However, don't focus just on the Q & A. Memorization is not our goal at MzeroA and it shouldn't be yours either. I NEVER advocate for someone to just remember the answers. I always want you to learn the WHY behind those answers.

Rote memorization will only get you so far and evaluators are experts at digging deeper. You must have a true understanding of the materials that the FAA requires you to know. I have included some scenario based questions with real world situations that are often asked so that you can put your knowledge to practical use.

This book will be your guide through the checkride process. If you use it well, it will ultimately help you to succeed.

Now let's get started on the path to Pass Your Private Pilot Checkride!

Contact us with ANY checkride questions. We are here to help!
Support@MzeroA.com | 855-737-1200

-Jason Schappert
Founder and President, MzeroA

Disclaimer

Our dedicated MzeroA team diligently collaborates each day to maintain the accuracy, accessibility, and timeliness of this book and all our educational materials. Our mission at MzeroA is to provide you with the finest study resources available.

At the time of publication, the information within this guide was thoroughly researched and verified for accuracy. However, it's important to acknowledge that regulations, FAA testing procedures, and technological advancements evolve continuously. Consequently, some information may become outdated in the months and years following publication.

Rest assured, we are committed to regularly updating and revising our study materials to reflect these changes. If you happen to identify an error, please don't hesitate to reach out to us. Keeping our resources current is a collaborative effort, and as a valued member of the MzeroA community, your input is invaluable.

In aviation, change is the only constant, as the saying goes. Therefore, we encourage you to utilize the latest editions of FAA resources, as they are regularly refreshed.

Your decision to entrust MzeroA with your Private Pilot Checkride preparation signifies more than just confidence — it signifies a partnership that we deeply cherish. Together, we are dedicated to ensuring your success on this monumental journey. Thank you for allowing us to be a part of realizing your dreams!

Acknowledgements

A huge thank you goes to the exceptional team at MzeroA, whose unwavering dedication and expertise have brought this latest edition of Pass Your Private Checkride to fruition. Your collective commitment to excellence and innovation sets a standard that inspires us all.

Together, we have redefined what it means to deliver top-tier educational materials. Your passion, drive, and relentless pursuit of perfection have made MzeroA synonymous with quality and reliability.

Thank you for your steadfast dedication to our mission and for being the backbone of our success.

Table of Contents

CHAPTER   **PAGE**

1. Certificates and Documents 15

2. Aeromedical Factors 25

3. Physical Weather 37

4. Textual Weather and Weather Services 47

5. Performance and Limitations 59

6. Flying at Night 73

7. Aircraft Systems 79

8. System Malfunctions & 91
   Emergency Procedures

9. Airspace 99

10. The National Transportation 113
    Safety Board (NTSB)

11. FAR/AIM 119

12. Cross Country Flight Planning 137

CHAPTER 1
CERTIFICATES AND DOCUMENTS

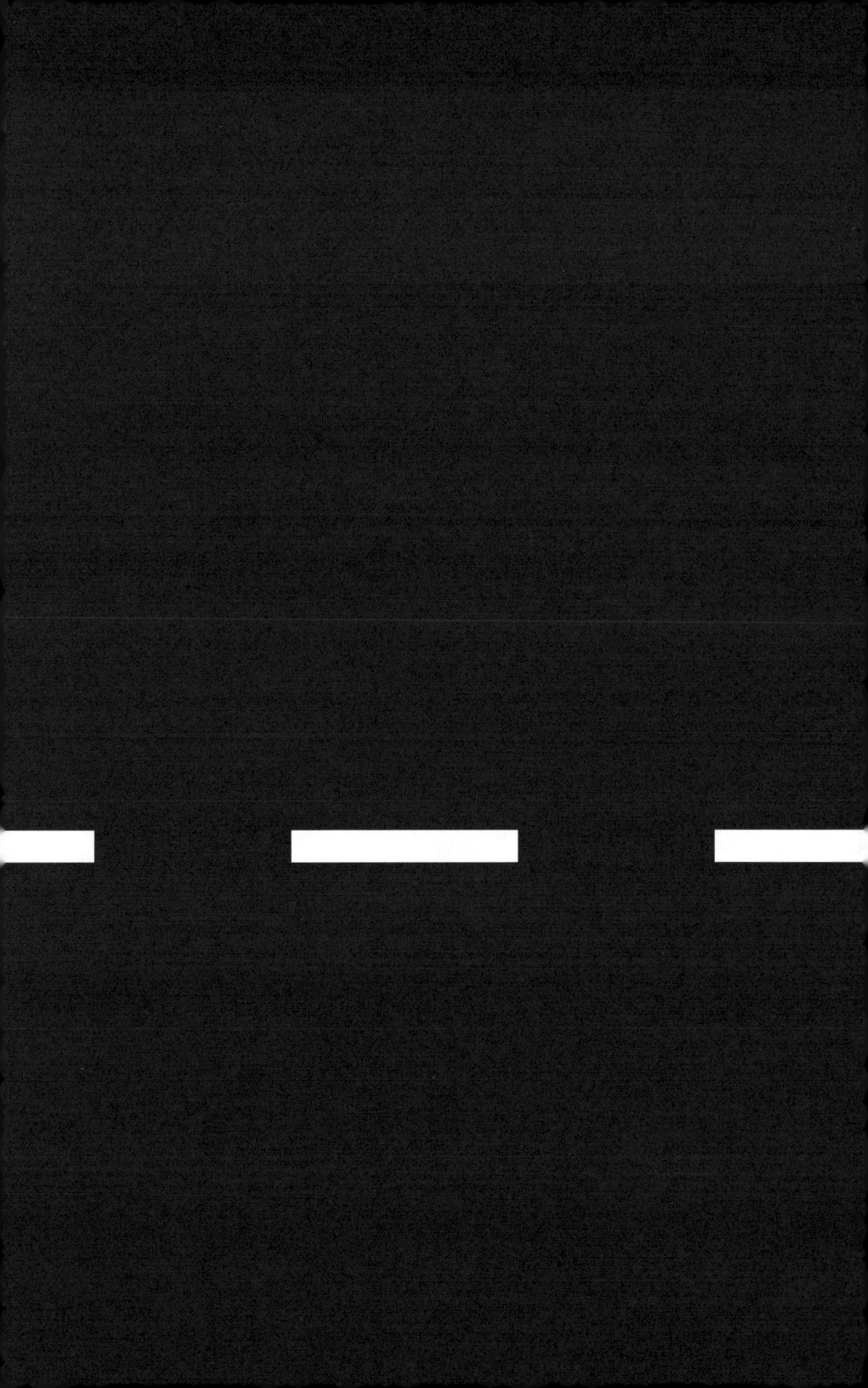

CHAPTER 1
Certificates and Documents

Most likely, the first area your checkride evaluator will ask questions is about pilot and airplane certificates and documents. You will be required to know the requirements and privileges of a Private Pilot Certificate. After all, this is what you are applying for, so naturally the evaluator will want to make sure you understand all aspects.

Know where to locate your airplane logbooks and documents. Be sure that you can point out inspection dates, which keep the airplane airworthy. Questions like these are very common on checkrides.

What is required to become a Private Pilot?

- You must be at least 17 years of age.
- Hold at least a current third class medical.
- Be able to read, write, and speak the English language.
- Pass the required knowledge test.
- Receive required ground and flight training endorsements.
- Meet aeronautical experience requirements for certificate.

> **A NOTE FROM JASON:**
>
> As you explain each of these, be sure to mention how you meet and exceed each one. For example, " I have to earn at least a 70% on my FAA Knowledge Test and I earned a 96%."

Source: 14 CFR 61.103

What are Private Pilot limitations and privileges?

Limitations:

1. Private Pilots may not pay less than pro rata share of the operating expenses of a flight with passengers. The expenses involved include: fuel, oil, airport expenditures, or rental fees.
2. Private Pilots cannot fly passengers or property for compensation or hire.

Privileges:

1. Private Pilots can demonstrate an aircraft to a prospective buyer as long as they are an aircraft salesperson or broker and have at least 200 hours of logged time.
2. Private Pilots may act as PIC (Pilot in Command) of an aircraft towing a glider or unpowered ultralight vehicle as long as they meet the requirements in 14 CFR 61.69.
3. Private Pilots may also act as PIC of an aircraft in connection with any business or employment if it is only incidental to that business or employment and does not carry passengers or property for compensation or hire.

Source: 14 CFR 61.113

How do you remain current as a Private Pilot?

Within the preceding 24 calendar months, you must complete a flight review. The flight review must be completed in an aircraft for which the pilot is rated by an authorized instructor and received a logbook endorsement certifying that the person has completed the review satisfactorily.

To remain current carrying passengers, a pilot must:

- Within the preceding 90 days, completed 3 takeoffs and landings as the sole manipulator of the flight controls in an aircraft of the same category and class and type rating if required.

- If the aircraft is conventional gear (tailwheel/taildragger), the landings must be to a full stop. If the passengers are to be carried at night the PIC must have made those 3 landings to a full stop during a period of 1 hour after sunset and 1 hour before sunrise.

Source: 14 CFR 61.56 & 61.57

What documents are required aboard the aircraft?

To help remember what documents are required aboard our aircraft at all times, use the acronym **SPARROW**.

- **S** - Supplements (example: G1000 supplement)
- **P** - Placards
- **A** - Airworthiness Certificate
- **R** - Registration Certificate
- **R** - Radio License (International Flights Only)
- **O** - Operating Limitations
- **W** - Weight and Balance Data

Source: 14 CFR 91.203 & 91.9

Does an aircraft registration expire?

Yes, every seven-years the owner must re-register their aircraft and send in the registration fee.

Source: FAA-H-8083–25

What documents must you have readily available while acting as Pilot in Command?

To act as PIC aboard an aircraft you must have:

- Photo ID
- Pilot Certificate (or Student Pilot Certificate)
- Medical*

A NOTE FROM JASON:

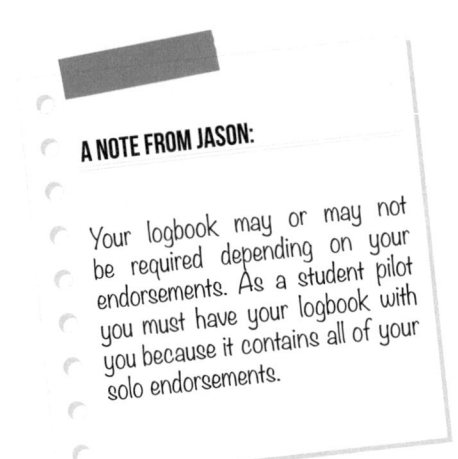

Your logbook may or may not be required depending on your endorsements. As a student pilot you must have your logbook with you because it contains all of your solo endorsements.

*Pilots must hold a FAA medical certificate unless operating under BasicMed. BasicMed is an alternative way for pilots to fly without a medical and the privileges include exercising student, recreational, and private pilot privileges when acting as PIC. I cover more about BasicMed in Chapter 2.

Source: 14 CFR 61.3

What inspections are required for your aircraft?

As a general rule, almost every aircraft can fall under the acronym "**AVIATES**"

- **A** - AD's (Airworthiness Directives)
- **V** - VOR check every 30 days (for IFR only)
- **I** - Inspections: Annual and 100 hour*
- **A** - Altimeter every 24 calendar months
- **T** - Transponder every 24 calendar months
- **E** - ELT every 12 calendar months
- **S** - Static System every 24 calendar months

Source: 14 CFR 91.409

* 100 Hour inspection is for aircraft flown for hire only.

What is the difference between a 100-hour and an Annual?

From a maintenance standpoint, a 100 hour and annual inspection follow the same scope of work. The difference is the time interval. If the aircraft is used for hire, then every 100 hours, the inspection has to be accomplished. An annual inspection must be completed yearly for all aircraft.

A favorite checkride question is "Can a 100 hour be substituted for an annual?" The answer is NO! However an annual CAN be substituted for a 100 hour.

What is a Progressive Inspection?

If authorized, some owners and operators choose to complete required inspections at different time intervals. The inspection schedule spreads out the required work needing to be performed over a period of time. This allows the aircraft to be back in service quicker than doing all the work at one time.

Source: 14 CFR 91.409

What is an MEL?

MEL stands for minimum equipment list. The best way to think of it is "The equipment that is allowed to be broken and the airplane can still legally be flown". When approved by the FAA, it allows aircraft to fly with certain inoperative instruments and equipment which are not essential for safe flight.

Source: AC 91-67, 14 CFR 91.213

What is a special flight permit?

A special flight permit may be issued to an aircraft that does not currently meet applicable airworthiness requirements. This is usually for a flight on a specific day, and to only one airport. To better explain this, here is an example:

My airplane is based at a private grass strip where there is no mechanic in the area. The annual inspection is overdue, therefore it is not airworthy. My local Flight Standards District Office (FSDO) grants me a special flight permit to fly it to an airport with a mechanic, If they deem the airplane is safe for flight.

Source: 14 CFR 21.197

What is the difference between maintenance and preventive maintenance?

The FAA defines the difference between the two types. Maintenance means inspection, overhaul, repair, preservation, and the replacement of parts, but excludes preventive maintenance. Preventive maintenance means simple or minor preservation operations and the replacement of small standard parts not involving complex assembly operations.

Source: 14 CFR 43 Appendix A

Can you as a private pilot perform preventive maintenance?

Yes! Except for holders of a sport pilot certificate, the holder of a pilot certificate issued under part 61 may perform preventive maintenance on any aircraft owned or operated by that pilot as long as it is not used under Part 121, 129, or 135. Keep in mind, just because you legally can do the work, doesn't mean that it's the best idea to do so. Maybe you are confident in replenishing the hydraulic fluid but not replacing spark plugs. Seek out an FAA authorized mechanic to help when needed. You can find a full list of items considered preventive maintenance in Part 43 of the FAA Regulations.

Source:14 CFR 43 Appendix A

CHAPTER 2
AEROMEDICAL FACTORS

CHAPTER 2
Aeromedical Factors

It is important that all pilots understand how our bodies act and react when in different situations. Pilots need to both pass a medical exam and understand that even though a pilot may hold a medical, there are situations that degrade a pilot's physical ability to operate an aircraft.

Let's first cover medicals.

Explain the three types of medicals.

1ST CLASS MEDICAL

- Highest and most extensive medical examination.
- Required if conducting a flight requiring an Airline Transport Pilot certificate for pilot in command privileges.

Duration:

For pilots aged 40 or older, the first class privileges expire for that operation at the end of the last day of the 6th month after the month of the date of examination shown on medical.

For pilots under age 40, the first class privileges expire for that operation at the end of the last day of the 12th month after the month of the date of examination shown on the medical certificate.

To be eligible for the first class medical certificate the applicant must meet these general requirements:

- Distant acuity of 20/20 in each eye, and near vision of 20/40.
- Ability to distinguish aviation red, aviation signal green, and white.

- Normal field of vision.
- Normal field of hearing.

2ND CLASS MEDICAL

- Required for pilots conducting flight as a Commercial Pilot.

Duration:

Second class privileges expire for that operation at the end of the 12th month after the month of the date of examination shown on the medical certificate for all pilots regardless of age.

To be eligible for the second class medical certificate the applicant must meet these general requirements:

- Distant acuity of 20/20 in each eye, and near vision of 20/40.
- Ability to distinguish aviation red, aviation signal green, and white.
- Normal field of vision.

3RD CLASS MEDICAL

- Required for all other pilot operations e.g. recreational pilot, private pilot, or flight instructor certificate.
- Most commonly held class medical in general aviation.

Duration:

For pilots aged 40 and older, third class privileges expire for that operation at the end of the last day of the 24th month after the month of the date of examination shown on the medical certificate.

For pilots under the age of 40, third class privileges expire for that operation at the end of the last day of the 60th month of the date of examination shown on the medical certificate.

To be eligible for the third class medical certificate the applicant must meet these general requirements:

- Distant acuity of 20/40 in each eye with or without corrective lenses, and near vision of 20/40.
- Ability to distinguish aviation red, aviation signal green, and white.
- Normal field of vision.
- Normal field of hearing.

Source: 14 CFR 61.23 and 14 CFR 61.53

A NOTE FROM JASON:

Please know that BasicMed is the biggest update to the FAA medical program. BasicMed states that if you've held at least a third class medical after July 14, 2006, have completed the online BasicMed course, and had your recommending physician complete the BasicMed questionnaire; you can fly aircraft up to 12,500 lbs, no higher than 18,000 feet MSL, no faster than 250 knots, with no more than 6 passengers, and never for compensation. Pilots operating under BasicMed must keep it current by passing a physical every 48 calendar months and retaking the online BasicMed course every 24 calendar months. Pilot examiners are now also allowed to conduct flight checks using BasicMed in aircraft that are covered by the BasicMed rule.

What is hypoxia?

Hypoxia is a lack of oxygen to the brain.

What are the four types of hypoxia?

- Hypoxic
- Stagnant
- Hypemic
- Histotoxic

Hypoxic hypoxia

This type of hypoxia is the most common and is caused by insufficient oxygen available to the body. If this happens, the person has less than 100% saturation of the blood in the arteries. This can commonly occur in pilots flying at an altitude where the oxygen content of air is low (e.g., over 12,500 feet).

Hypemic hypoxia

This type of hypoxia is caused by the reduction of the oxygen carrying capacity of the blood. Anemia (low hemoglobin) and carbon monoxide poisoning can cause this type of hypoxia. The oxygen is available, but there isn't enough good blood to carry the oxygen. The body's red blood cells take in carbon monoxide much faster than oxygen. Therefore, not enough oxygen gets transported throughout the body. Smoking cigarettes and exhaust leaks in your airplane engine are common examples of how carbon monoxide poisoning may occur in pilots.

Stagnant hypoxia

This type of hypoxia is caused by reduced cardiac output (the pump isn't working well enough!) or by venous pooling during high G force stresses. In simple terms, blood is not flowing for some reason to all parts of the body. During flight, stagnant hypoxia can occur when under a G force. This is why aerobatic pilots wear G-suits to help minimize the effects.

Histotoxic hypoxia

This occurs when all systems are working but the cells can't absorb the available oxygen in the blood. Alcohol or drug use and poisoning can cause this type of hypoxia.

Source: Pilot's Handbook of Aeronautical Knowledge

What are some symptoms of hypoxia?

- Headache
- Dizziness/Lightheaded
- Cyanosis (blue lips or fingertips)
- Euphoria
- Fatigue
- Tingling or numbness in the body
- Decreased response time
- Impaired judgment
- Visual impairment
- Drowsiness

Everybody reacts differently while in a hypoxic state and may not have the same or all symptoms as another person.

Explain Hyperventilation.

Hyperventilation is having an excessive breathing rate, which leads to abnormal loss of carbon dioxide. Hyperventilation can also be called "over-breathing." The person is breathing at too rapid of a rate and as they exhale, the carbon dioxide in their blood exits with each exhale.

Usually caused by panic or stress, the best cure is to breathe into a bag or talk aloud to help regulate breathing. The most obvious sign of hyperventilation is rapid breathing. Other common symptoms are similar to those of hypoxia, so it is important to diagnose properly. Dizziness, visual impairment, tingling sensations, and unconsciousness are some symptoms shared with hypoxia.

What is spatial disorientation, and what are the different types?

Spatial disorientation is the state of confusion where the pilot loses visual reference, or orientation to the actual horizon.

The Leans

The leans occur when there is a sudden return to level flight from a slow prolonged turn that went unnoticed by the pilot. The sensors in your inner ear sends your brain the sensation of banking in the opposite direction. Therefore, the pilot may lean in the direction of the original turn.

Coriolis Illusion

The Coriolis Illusion is caused by making a quick head movement during a constant rate turn that has ceased stimulating the inner ear. The most common occurrence of this is when a pilot making an extended turn, drops a pen, approach plate etc, and moves his or her head in a different direction which sends the fluid in the ear canal moving in an entirely different axis. A disoriented pilot may put the airplane into a dangerous attitude. It is best to avoid abrupt head movements while under IFR.

Graveyard Spin

Prolonged spins can give the pilot the sensation that the spin is progressively decreasing. Therefore, when the pilot applies opposite rudder to counteract the spin, that input may cause a pilot to wrongly sense a spin in the opposite direction. If the pilot responds with rudder correction to the illusion created, the airplane will reenter the original spin.

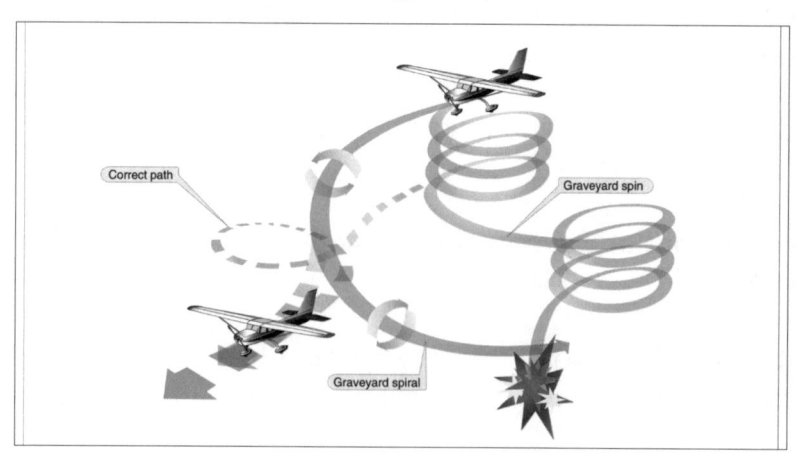

Graveyard Spiral

In this illusion, a pilot may experience the illusion of not turning after being in a constant rate turn for an extended period of time. Returning to straight and level flight causes the sensation of turning so the pilot turns back into the original turn. While turning, the pilot notices a loss of altitude but does not recognize that the aircraft is in a turn. The sensory system makes the pilot feel as though in level flight so he or she pitches back. The abrupt pitching back tightens the turn and you lose even more altitude.

Somatogravic Illusion

This illusion usually occurs during takeoff. The rapid acceleration pushes the pilot back in his or her seat, giving them the sensation of a nose up attitude. Because of this feeling, the pilot incorrectly pushes the nose of the aircraft downward.

Note: A rapid deceleration has the opposite effect.

Inversion Illusion

A quick change from a climb to level flight makes the pilot feel as though he or she is tumbling backwards. The natural tendency is to nose the aircraft over, which actually intensifies the illusion.

Elevator Illusion

On a turbulent day, an updraft could cause extreme vertical acceleration and the pilot may nose over the aircraft. This illusion also has the opposite effect with downdrafts.

False Horizon

A false horizon can be caused by city lights, sloping clouds, stars, or darkness. The pilot believes that the false horizon is the real horizon and tries to align the aircraft with it, placing the aircraft in this dangerous attitude.

Autokinesis

At night or in darkness, when a light is stared at for a long period of time it begins to appear to move. While flying at night, pilots should not stare at stationary lights for long periods of time to avoid this sensation.

True Story from Jason:

> I remember a flight I made shortly after earning my private pilot certificate. I needed to make a trip from Ocala to Tallahassee. Because it was the only plane available in the coming days for a flight, I was checked out in the school's brand new G1000 Cessna 172. The G1000 checkout was less than an hour and covered the basics of the system. My flight to Tallahassee was easy and uneventful. However, the event I was attending ran long which meant I would be unexpectedly flying home at night. Even though my entire night flying experience only included the three required night hours to earn my private pilot, coupled with the fact that I was in a "new to me" airplane at an unfamiliar airport, I decided to depart for home. After departure into the dark sky, I realized no one ever taught me how to dim those bright G1000 screens. This was an original Non-WASS G1000 that wasn't capable of auto dimming yet. As I reached my cruising altitude, spatial disorientation began to set in. With no moon, the Gulf of Mexico to my right, and featureless terrain ahead I began to feel as though the airplane was turning. But my VERY bright G1000 (which wasn't helping the outside visual picture) said otherwise. For that entire flight home I spoke aloud the words "trust your instruments." It became my mantra as I said it over and over. I made it safely back to Ocala that night but learned a new healthy respect for night flying and the illusions associated with spatial disorientation.

I put together an easy acronym to help you remember the types of spatial disorientation come checkride day and beyond. The acronym is **ICEFLAGS**:

- **I** - Inversion Illusion
- **C** - Coriolis Illusion
- **E** - Elevator Illusion
- **F** - False Horizon
- **L** - Leans
- **A** - Autokinesis
- **G** - Graveyard Spin/Spiral
- **S** - Somatogravic Illusion

CHAPTER 3
PHYSICAL WEATHER

CHAPTER 3
Physical Weather

Understanding weather is important for pilots! At times, weather patterns can assist pilots like when you have a tailwind. At other times, weather can be the reason the flight has to be canceled or delayed. In order to make good decisions, we need to know answers to questions like "What causes thunderstorms? What's a front? What causes turbulence?" Physical weather is required not only to pass the private pilot knowledge and practical tests, but for real world flying.

What causes weather to occur?

Heat Exchange. The Sun hits the Earth unevenly which causes differences in temperature. The physical process of weather is a result of this unequal heating.

What is standard temperature and pressure?

- 15°C (59°F)
- 29.92 inches of mercury, 1013.2 Hg (hectopascals)

What are the 3 main layers of the atmosphere in which weather occurs?

- The Troposphere (closest to the Earth, vast majority of weather events occurs within it).
- The Tropopause (top layer of Troposphere, associated with the jet stream and clear air turbulence).
- The Stratosphere (few weather events exist here).

What causes wind?

Wind is caused by air flowing from high to low pressure areas.

Name and explain the four main types of fog:

- Radiation Fog
- Advection Fog
- Upslope Fog
- Steam Fog

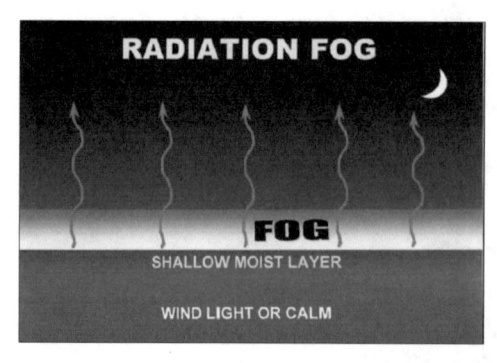

Radiation Fog

Radiation fog is a result of rapid drop in ground temperature, which causes surface air to cool faster than in higher altitudes. Because of this, radiation fog can be encountered only during clear skies with minimal wind activity and a small temperature-dew point spread.

Advection Fog

Advection fog is the result of the movement of moist air over cool surfaces, particularly near coastal areas. The colder temperature of the surface causes moisture to condense and become fog.

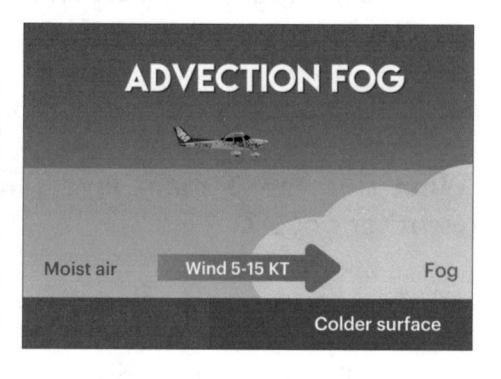

Upslope Fog

When warm moist air is carried by the wind up sloping terrain, forming upslope fog.

Steam Fog

Steam fog often occurs in Fall or Winter when cold air moves over relatively warmer water. Moisture evaporates from the water surface to produce saturation. As the rising water vapor meets the colder air above, it re-condenses creating a fog which appears to rise from the water surface. This type of fog is associated with unstable air and therefore will often be an area of convective turbulence.

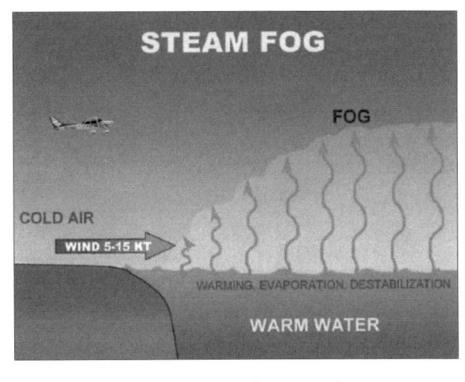

What are the characteristics of stable air?

Stratiform clouds, continuous precipitation, smooth air, and fair to poor visibility in haze and smoke.

What are the characteristics of unstable air?

Cumulus clouds, showery precipitation, good visibility, strong surface winds and turbulence.

What is the difference between an air mass and a front?

Air mass – A large body of air with generally uniform temperature and humidity. The area from which an air mass originates is called a source region.

Front – A boundary separating two air masses of different densities, temperature and humidity. A front is the principal cause of meteorological phenomena.

What are the four types of fronts?

- Cold Front
- Warm Front
- Stationary Front
- Occluded Front

Cold Front – Leading edge of colder air that is replacing warmer air.

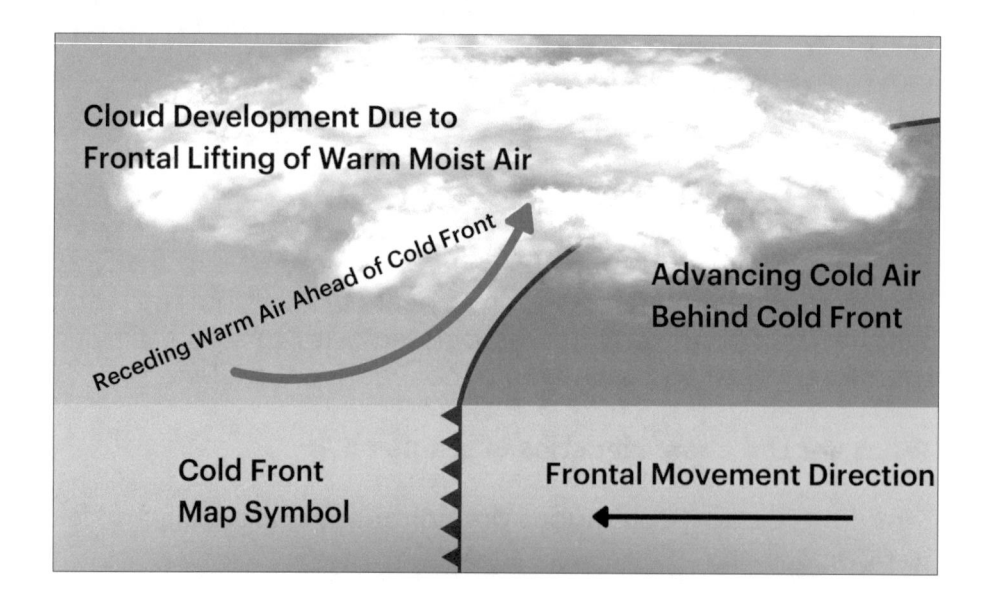

Cloud Development Due to Frontal Lifting of Warm Moist Air

Receding Warm Air Ahead of Cold Front

Advancing Cold Air Behind Cold Front

Cold Front Map Symbol

Frontal Movement Direction

Warm Front – Leading edge of warmer air that is replacing cooler air.

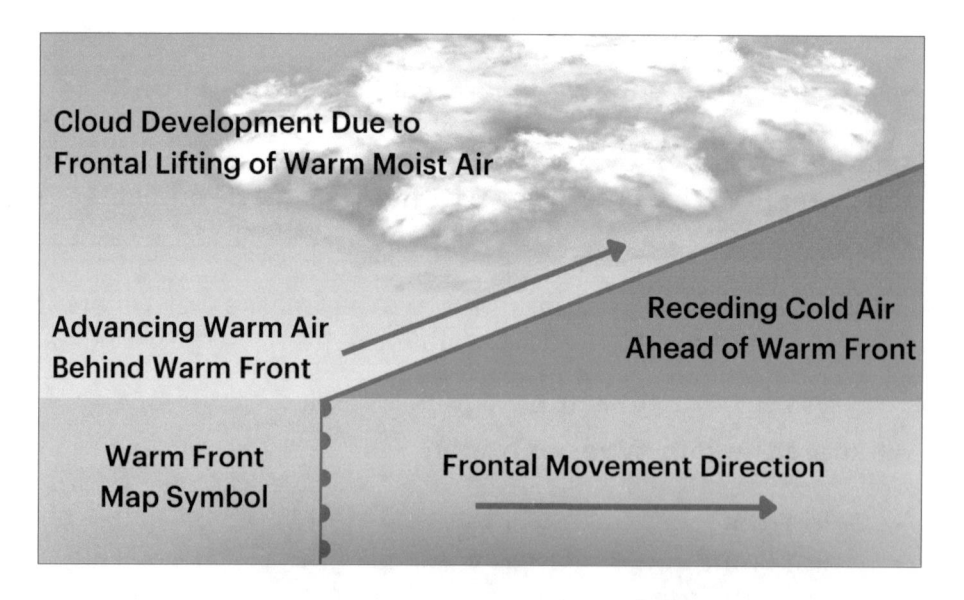

Cloud Development Due to Frontal Lifting of Warm Moist Air

Advancing Warm Air Behind Warm Front

Receding Cold Air Ahead of Warm Front

Warm Front Map Symbol

Frontal Movement Direction

Stationary Front – A front with little movement.

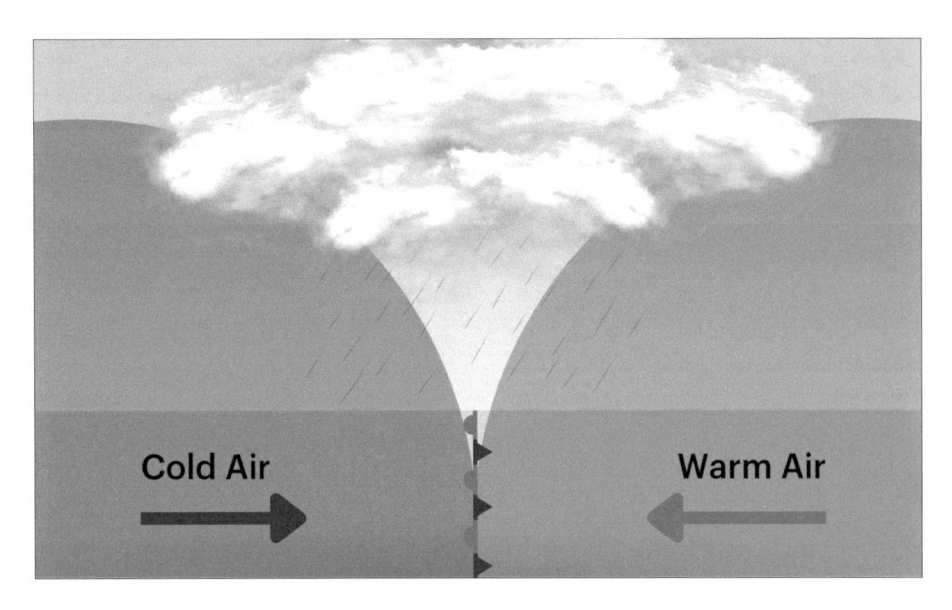

Cold Air

Warm Air

Occluded Front – When a cold front catches up to a warm front.

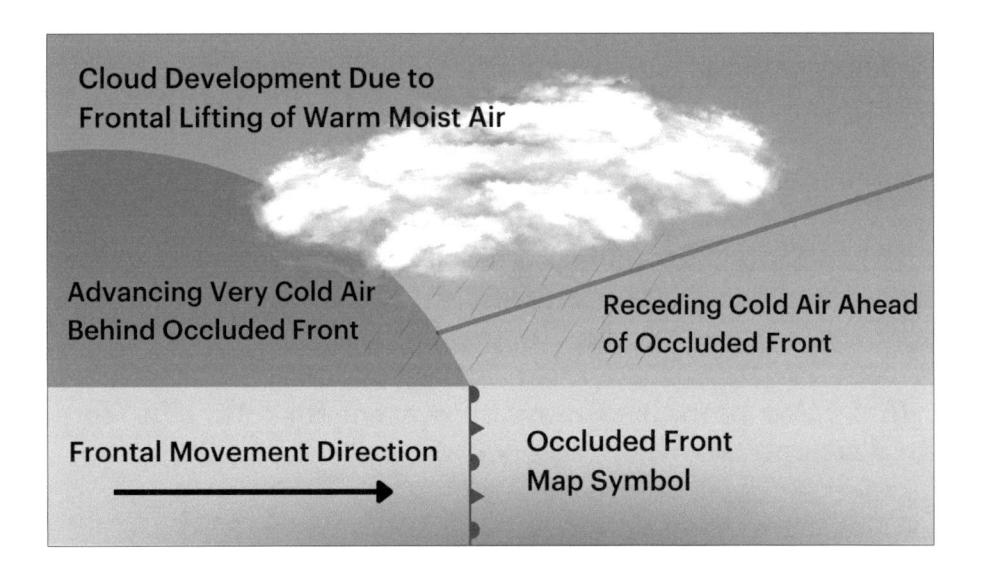

Cloud Development Due to Frontal Lifting of Warm Moist Air

Advancing Very Cold Air Behind Occluded Front

Receding Cold Air Ahead of Occluded Front

Frontal Movement Direction

Occluded Front Map Symbol

What causes turbulence?

- Convective currents (convective turbulence)
- Obstructions in wind flow (mechanical turbulence)
- Wind shear

Source: AC 00-06

What are the three types of structural icing?

- Clear Ice
- Rime Ice
- Mixed Ice

Clear Ice

Clear and hard, it forms by relatively slow freezing large supercooled water droplets.

Rime Ice

Brittle and opaque, it is formed by small water drops of precipitation that freeze rapidly before spreading across the airfoil.

Mixed Ice

Hard and rough, it is a mixture of both clear and rime ice and forms as a result water droplets varying in size, temperature, and water content collect on the airplane.

What three properties must be present for a thunderstorm to develop?

- Sufficient water vapor
- An unstable lapse rate
- Uplifting (to start the process in motion)

What are the three stages of a thunderstorm?

1. **Cumulus Stage:** characterized by initial updrafts.
2. **Mature Stage:** characterized by the beginning of falling precipitation.
3. **Dissipating Stage:** characterized by large downdrafts.

Due to the hazards associated with thunderstorms, the FAA recommends avoiding them by what distance?

20 miles. If flying between intense or extreme echos, pilots should ensure 40 miles separation between them to safely navigate past them. Hail and hazardous turbulence may extend to as much as 20 miles from the echo edge!

What are isobars?

Isobars are lines depicted on a weather chart that show areas of equal pressure.

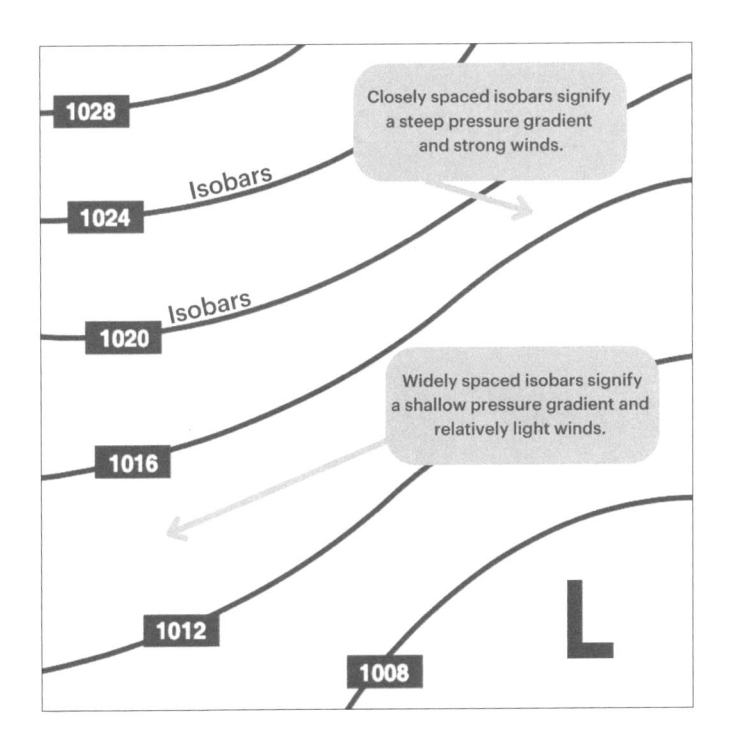

CHAPTER 4
TEXTUAL WEATHER AND WEATHER SERVICES

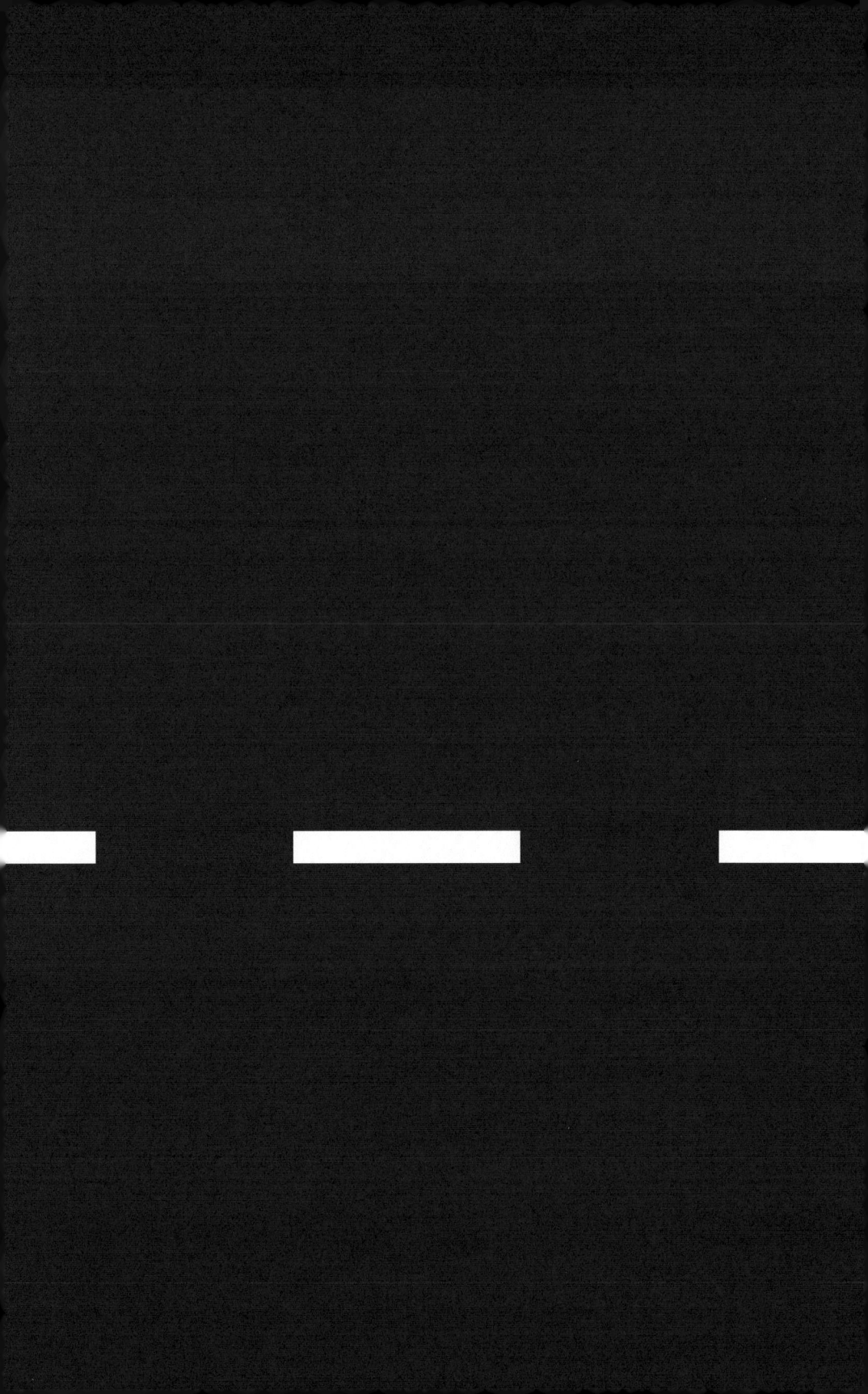

CHAPTER 4
Textual Weather and Weather Services

Reading METARS, TAFS, and PIREPS can take time to understand and may seem like a foreign language early in training because of the many codes. However, this chapter was designed with simplicity in mind. We break down what it all means and include some practice examples for you to decode. Use this section to review and fine-tune your textual weather knowledge.

METARS

How long are METARs valid?

An hour, unless an amended or special METAR replaces it.

When are they normally issued?

55 minutes past the hour.

Practice decoding this METAR:

METAR KJFK 242235Z 28024G36KT 7SM -RA BR BKN009 OVC020CB 26/24 A2998 RMK AO2 SLP993 T02640238 56012

KJFK – Station ID

242235Z – Prepared on the 24th day of the month at 2235 Zulu (UTC)

28024G36KT – Winds are from 280 at 24 Knots Gusting to 36 Knots

7SM – Visibility 7 Statute Miles

-RA BR – Light Rain (-RA) Mist (BR)

BKN009 OVC020CB – Ceiling 900 feet Broken, 2,000ft Overcast, Cumulonimbus

26/24 – Temperature 26 degrees C, dew point 24 degrees C

A2998 – Altimeter 29.98

RMK – Remarks

AO2 – Station has automatic precipitation discriminator.

SLP993 – Sea level pressure 999.3 hectopascals (add either a "9" or "10" to the front, whichever makes the number closest to 1,000).

T02640238 – Exact Temperature 26.4, Exact Dewpoint 23.8.

56012 – Atmospheric Pressure is lower than 3 hours ago ("5" means Atmospheric Pressure. If the next number is a 1,2, or 3 the Atmospheric Pressure has increased since the previous 3 hours. 4 means it has stayed the same. A 5,6,7,8 means that it has decreased. In this case, the 6 indicates that it has decreased and done so by .12 or 12%. This section tends to be difficult to decode for many pilots.

> **A NOTE FROM JASON:**
> Reading METARS is tough! The METAR example listed here is the actual METAR that I decoded on my CFI checkride. When I was teaching the last segment (56012) regarding the atmospheric pressure, the checkride examiner looked at me and said "Wow, I never knew that's what that meant!"
> This story goes to show that no one has all the answers, but being able to know where to find answers is key. A good pilot is always learning!

Quick Weather Guide with List of Terms and Symbols

(-) Light Intensity	**GR** Hail
(No symbol) Moderate Intensity	**GS** Small Hail and/or Snow Pellets
(+) Heavy Intensity	**FG** Fog
VC In the Vicinity	**FU** Smoke
MI Shallow	**VA** Volcanic Ash
PR Partial	**DU** Widespread Dust
BC Patches	**SA** Sand
DR Low Drifting	**HZ** Haze
BL Blowing	**PO** Well-Developed Dust/ Sand Whirls
SH Shower(s)	**FC** Funnel Cloud
TS Thunderstorm	**+FC** Tornado/ Waterspout
FZ Freezing	**SS** Sand storm
DZ Drizzle	**DS** Dust storm
RA Rain	**UP** Unknown Precipitation
SN Snow	**PY** Spray
SG Snow Grains	**SQ** Squalls
IC Ice Crystals	
PL Ice Pellets	
BR Mist	

TAFS

How long are TAFs valid?

Usually 24 hours.

How often are TAFs issued?

4 times daily.

Practice decoding this TAF:

KATL 151603Z 1516/1618 24008KT P6SM SCT035
TEMPO 1518/1522 4SM -TSRA BKN030CB
FM160200 23006KT P6SM SCT060 BKN100

KATL – TAF for Atlanta

151603Z – Issued On the 15th day of the month at 1603Z

1516/1618 – TAF is valid from the 15th day of the month at 1600Z to the 16th day of the month at 1800Z

24008KT – Wind from 240 degrees at 8 knots

P6SM – Visibility is greater than 6 statute miles (remember it by saying Plus 6 statute miles)

SCT035 – Scattered clouds at 3,500 feet

TEMPO 1518/1522 – Temporarily from the 15th at 1800Z to the 15th at 2200Z these will be the conditions

4SM – 4 Statute Miles of visibility

-TSRA - Thunderstorms (TS) and light (-) Rain (RA)

BKN030CB – Broken clouds 3,000 feet Cumulonimbus (CB)

FM160200 – From the 16th at 0200Z these will be the conditions

23006KT – Wind from 230 degrees at 6 knots

P6SM – Visibility greater than 6 statute miles
SCT060 – Scattered clouds 6,000 feet

BKN100 – Broken clouds 10,000 feet

Note: The first line of the TAF after the date of issuance and validity times shares what the conditions are generally expected to be over the forecasted time.

On the Forecast you will see one of the following:

FM (time) – The From group, the group most commonly seen, shows a rapid or significant change occurring in less than 1 hour.

TEMPO (time) – The temporary group is used to show fluctuations of wind, visibility, or sky conditions expected to last for LESS THAN 1 hour, and expected to occur during half of the given time period.

PROB30 stands for probability, the 30 indicates a 30% chance the conditions could happen.

ex: PROB30 1018/1021 2SM TSRA BKN025CB – There is a 30% chance that on the 10th day between 1800Z and 2100Z the visibility could drop to 2 statute miles due to Rain and Thunderstorms, the ceiling could be as low as Broken at 2,500 feet with cumulonimbus clouds.

PIREPS

When are they issued?

PIREPs are issued when given by pilots. Most often, pilots will give a PIREP when encountering unforecasted or worse than forecasted weather conditions.

Required data found in all PIREP's are as follows:

UA - Routine or uua – urgent
OV - Location of the PIREP
TM - Time the PIREP was received from the pilot
FL - Flight level or altitude above sea level of the PIREP
TP - Type of aircraft

Optional info to be reported and displayed:

SK - Sky cover
TA - Temperature
WV - Wind velocity
TB - Turbulence
IC - Icing
RM - Remarks

Practice decoding this PIREP:

UA /OV YSP 090025 /TM 2120 /FL050 /TP BE99 /SK 020BKN040 110OVC /TA -14 /WV 030045 /TB MDT CAT 060-080 /IC LGT RIME 020-040 /RM LGT FZRA INC

It reads as follows:

Aircraft observation was east of the Marathon, Ontario VOR/DME from 90 degrees at 25 NM at 2120 UTC. The aircraft was at 5,000 feet and is a Beech 19. The clouds were broken at 2,000 feet MSL, with tops at 4,000 feet, and an overcast layer at 11,000 feet MSL. The temperature is -14 degrees celsius and the winds are from 030 at 45 knots. There is moderate clear air turbulence between 6,000 feet and 8,000 feet. There is light rime icing between 2,000 feet and 4,000 feet.

Note: This would indicate that the icing is picked up in the cloud. The remarks section says that light freezing rain was encountered in the cloud.

What is a low level prognostic chart?

The low level significant weather prognostic chart is different from other charts in that it is a forecast chart (not an observation chart). The "prog" chart is issued four times daily and provides a 12-hour and a 24-hour weather forecast for a given region. It also only covers from the surface up to the 400- millibar pressure level (24,000 feet in altitude). It is to be used only in planning flights below 24,000 feet. It is one of the more widely used because of its ease to read.

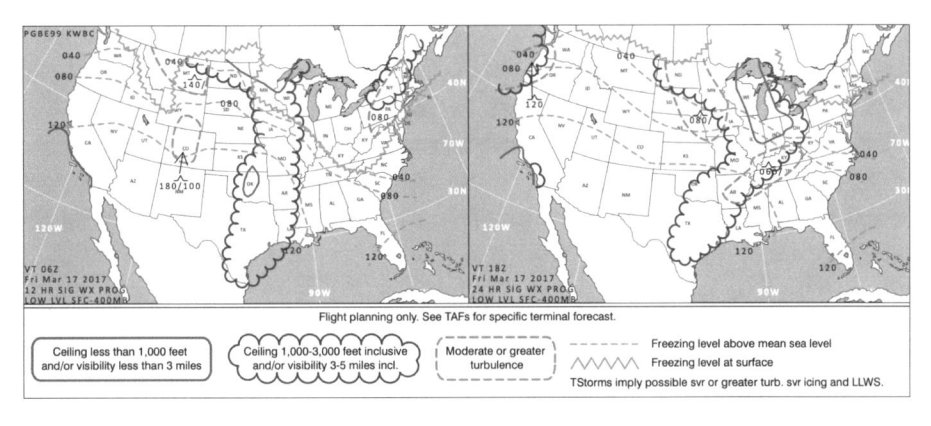

What is a Surface Analysis Chart?

Surface Analysis Chart (or Surface Weather Chart) depicts the weather conditions as they were a few hours earlier to the time stamped on the chart. These charts are developed every 3 hours. Reviewing this chart gives a picture of atmospheric pressure patterns, locations of high and low pressure systems as well as frontal movements.

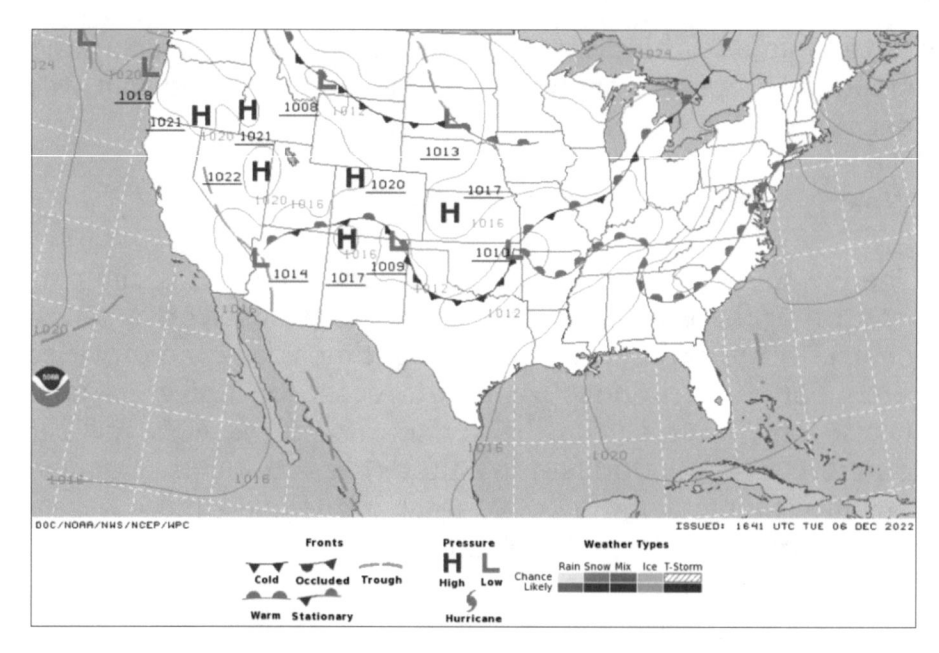

What is a Graphical Forecast for Aviation (GFA)?

A GFA is a tool used to show a complete picture of observed and forecasted weather information all in one source. The information, is laid out over a map of the United States.

Define AIRMET, SIGMET and Convective SIGMET.

AIRMET

Information on weather conditions which may be hazardous to light aircraft. AIRMETs include information on moderate icing or turbulence, sustained winds of 30 knots or more at the surface, widespread IFR conditions, and extensive mountain obscurement.

SIGMET

Information on weather conditions potentially hazardous to all types of aircraft. A SIGMET implies severe icing, severe or greater turbulence, widespread sandstorms, widespread dust storms, or volcanic ash.

Convective SIGMET

A convective SIGMET will be issued for thunderstorms. Any Convective SIGMET also implies severe or greater turbulence, severe icing, and low-level windshear.

What are the three types of AIRMETS?

AIRMET Tango – Turbulence and surface winds greater than 30 knots.

AIRMET Sierra – IFR conditions or mountain obstructions.

AIRMET Zulu – Icing conditions.

What is a Center Weather Advisory?

CWAs (Center Weather Advisories) are issued by control centers and concern both SIGMET and AIRMET type conditions described in greater detail and related to a specific ARTCC area.

Define the term ceiling.

Ceiling means the height above the earth's surface of the lowest layer of clouds reported as broken (BKN), overcast (OVC), or obscuration.

CHAPTER 5
PERFORMANCE AND LIMITATIONS

CHAPTER 5
Performance and Limitations

When pilots calculate airplane performance and limitations, there is a lot to consider. It includes subjects such as, but not limited, to aerodynamics, weight and balance, weather, and density altitude. This chapter will help you better understand your airplane and why it performs the way it does.

What are the four forces that act on an airplane?

- Lift
- Weight
- Thrust
- Drag

What is "Angle of Attack"?

The acute angle between the chord line of an airfoil and the direction of the air that strikes the airfoil (relative wind).

What is relative wind?

The direction of airflow with respect to an airfoil. It is parallel and opposite the path of the airfoils movement.

What is Bernoulli's Principle of Differential Pressure?

Bernoulli's Principle explains lift. The pressure of a liquid or gas varies with its speed of motion. As velocity increases, pressure decreases. This explains what is occurring as air moves over and under the wing.

A wing shape, known as an airfoil, is generally slightly curved on the top and flat on the bottom. This curvature causes air to travel faster over the wing's top than its bottom. A lower pressure will occur on the top of the wing, compared to a higher pressure on the bottom of the wing. Pressure moves from high to low, causing lift.

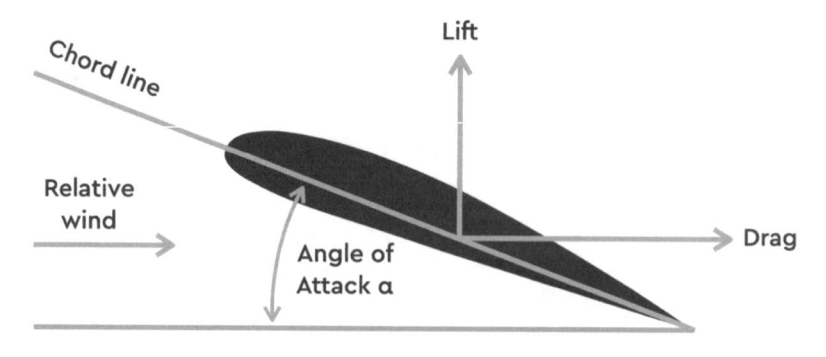

Diagram: Airfoil cross-section showing Chord line, Relative wind, Angle of Attack α, Lift, and Drag.

What is an aerodynamic stall?

An aerodynamic stall results when smooth airflow over the wing is disrupted by exceeding the critical angle of attack. The smooth airflow over the wing is disrupted and needed lift is lost.

What are the characteristics of an aft CG and forward CG?

	Aft CG	**Forward CG**
Stability	Less stable because the center of gravity is closer to the center of pressure, which causes longitudinal instability. It also makes stall and spin recovery more difficult	More stable because the center of gravity is further from the center of pressure. This increases longitudinal stability
Cruise Speed	Higher cruise speed due to reduced drag and smaller angle of attack required to maintain altitude	Slower cruise speed due to increased drag and greater angle of attack required to maintain altitude
Stall Speed	Lower stall speed because there is less wing loading	Higher stall speed due to increased wing loading. Our critical angle of attack is reached at a higher speed

What is P-Factor?

P-Factor (propeller factor) involves Newton's Third Law of Motion; for every action, there is an equal and opposite reaction. Typically, the propeller rotates clockwise from pilot's seat, causing the airplane to rotate oppositely. Right rudder application during climbs or with full power compensates for P-Factor.

What is drag?

Drag is the force that opposes airplane movement through the air. Drag is defined as an aerodynamic force that resists the motion of an object moving through a fluid (air and water are both fluids). If you stick your hand out of a car window while moving, you will experience a very simple demonstration of this effect. The amount of drag that your hand creates depends on a few factors, such as the size of your hand, the speed of the car and the density of the air. If you were to slow down, you would notice that the drag on your hand would decrease.

What are the two types of drag?

Parasite Drag

This drag is caused by displacement of air by the aircraft movement. The three types of parasite drag are skin, form, and interference drag.

Induced Drag

Induced drag is a by-product of lift, generated by an airfoil passing through the air.

What is load factor?

Load factor is the ratio of the lift generated by the wings at any given time, divided by the total weight of the aircraft.

It represents the load supported by the wings, divided by the aircraft's total weight.

Define maneuvering speed (Va).

The max speed at which abrupt control deflections or maneuvers can be performed and not over stress the airplane. Flying at or below Va will allow the airplane to stall before exceeding allowable G forces.

The formula for calculating maneuvering speed is:

$$\text{Va at current weight} = (\text{Va at max weight}) \sqrt{\frac{\text{weight}}{\text{max weight}}}$$

What is the relationship between maneuvering speed and weight?

Maneuvering speed decreases as the weight of the aircraft decreases, because the effects of aerodynamic forces become more pronounced.

What causes a spin?

The airplane being put into a stall is the cause of a spin. When the pilot does not correct stall conditions, a spin may occur. Both wings are stalled in a spin. However, one wing is stalled more than the other which causes a corkscrew spinning motion.

What are the general steps in spin recovery?

The acronym to use is P.A.R.E.

- **P** - Power to idle.
- **A** - Ailerons neutral.
- **R** - Rudder full in the opposite direction of the spin.
- **E** - Elevator forward (Remember the airplane is still stalled).

When are spins most likely to occur?

A stall must happen for a spin to occur. Therefore, a spin may develop anytime during flight where you meet or exceed the critical angle of attack and enter a stalled condition.

Define ground effect.

When an aircraft is flying very close to the ground, the drag resulting from the creation of lift is reduced. The ground or water surface causes a change in the airflow over the wing reducing drag. It affects a low-winged aircraft more than a mid-or high-winged aircraft because its wings are closer to the ground.

What is adverse yaw?

A flight condition where the nose of an aircraft tends to turn away from the intended direction of turn.

Define these weight and balance related terms:

Standard Empty Weight

The weight of the airframe and engine with all standard equipment installed. It also includes the unusable fuel and oil.

Optional or Extra Equipment

Any and all additional instruments, radio equipment, etc., installed but not included as standard equipment, the weight of which is added to the standard weight to get the basic empty weight. It also includes fixed ballast, full engine coolant, hydraulic and deicing fluid.

Basic Empty Weight

The weight of the airplane with all optional equipment included. In most modern airplanes, the manufacturer includes full oil in the basic empty weight.

Useful load

The difference between gross takeoff weight and basic empty weight. It is, in other words, all the load which is removable, which is not permanently part of the airplane. It includes the usable fuel, the pilot, crew, passengers, baggage, freight, etc.

Payload

The load available as passengers, baggage, freight, etc, after the weight of pilot, crew, usable fuel have been deducted from the useful load.

Operational Empty Weight

The basic empty weight of the airplane plus the weight of the pilot. It excludes payload and usable fuel.

Usable Fuel

Fuel available for flight planning.

Unusable Fuel

Fuel remaining in the tanks after a run-out test has been completed according to federal regulations.

Maximum Gross Weight

The maximum permissible weight of the airplane.

Maximum Takeoff Weight

The maximum weight approved at the start of the takeoff run.

Maximum Ramp Weight

The maximum weight approved for ground maneuvering. It includes the weight of fuel used for start, taxi and run up.

Zero Fuel Weight

The weight of the airplane, exclusive of usable fuel.

Passenger Weights

The weight of your passengers.

Complete the following weight shift problem.

An airplane takes off at 3,000 lbs and a CG at station 60. Since takeoff 25 gal (150 lbs) of fuel has been consumed. The fuel CG is at station 65, find the new CG.

Here's the formula used:

$$M1 \pm \Delta M \text{ divided by } W1 \pm \Delta W$$

$$\frac{M1 \pm \Delta M}{W1 \pm \Delta W}$$

Which translates to this: Our original moment (M1) plus or minus our change in moment (ΔM) divided by our original weight (W1) plus or minus our change in weight (ΔW).
So apply the numbers in our question above to the formula:

$$\frac{(3000 \times 60) - (150 \times 65)}{3{,}000 - 150} = 59.74$$

New CG station is at 59.74 inches.

$$(3000 \times 60) - (150 \times 65) / 3{,}000 - 150 = 59.74$$

New CG station is at 59.74 inches.

Explain the Different Types of Altitude:

Indicated Altitude

Altitude read right off the altimeter when it's set to the correct local altimeter setting.

True Altitude

The actual height above sea level.

Absolute Altitude

The actual height above the terrain.

Pressure Altitude

Read on the altimeter when set to 29.92.

Density Altitude

Pressure altitude corrected for nonstandard temperature.

What is density altitude?

As written above, density altitude is best defined as pressure altitude corrected for nonstandard temperature variations. What it means for our airplane is that when the air is less dense it reduces airplane performance. Ever wonder why our airplane performs better some days more than others? It all comes down to density altitude. Low air density results in high density altitude. High air density results in low density altitude.

How do you calculate density altitude?

If you know pressure altitude, density altitude can be calculated on your E6B or electronic flight computer. However, I always use the following formula.

Density Altitude = Pressure Altitude + (OAT - Standard Temp) x 120

Note: OAT = Outside Air Temperature

For example:
PA = 600
OAT = 19
Standard Temp = 15
600 + (19-15) x 120 = 1,080 feet

So your airplane "feels" like it's at 1,080 feet just sitting on the ground.

What factors affect density altitude?

Humidity

A high humidity will increase density altitude. The water vapor is a gas and takes up space in the atmosphere. The water vapor when mixed with oxygen will make the air less dense.

Temperature

Remember, the warmer the air gets the less dense it becomes. This is why our airplane always performs better in the winter months. Warm air decreases performance because it increases density altitude.

Altitude

This one should be a given. We know that at higher altitude the air is less dense, which means a decrease in airplane performance.

Define the following V Speeds:

V_A	-	Design maneuvering speed
V_{FE}	-	Maximum flaps extended speed
V_{LE}	-	Maximum landing gear-extended speed
V_{LO}	-	Maximum landing gear-operating speed
V_{NE}	-	Never exceed speed
V_{NO}	-	Maximum structural cruising speed
V_{SO}	-	Stalling speed in the landing configuration
V_{S1}	-	Stalling speed in the clean configuration
V_X	-	Best angle of climb
V_Y	-	Best rate of climb

A NOTE FROM JASON:

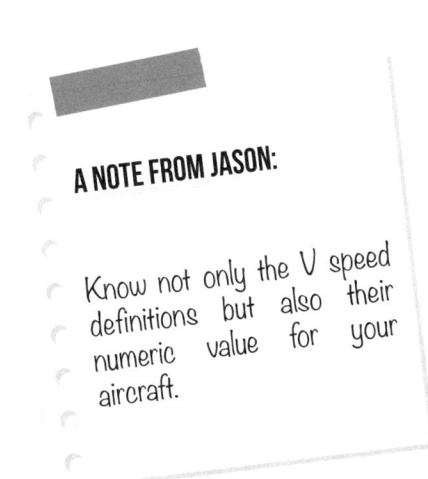

Know not only the V speed definitions but also their numeric value for your aircraft.

Define the following airspeeds:

Indicated airspeed (IAS)

Read directly from the airspeed indicator.

Calibrated airspeed (CAS)

Indicated airspeed corrected for installation error and instrument error.

True Airspeed (TAS)

Actual speed of an aircraft moving through the air. The airspeed indicator displays TAS only at sea level under standard conditions, so you must calculate TAS based on IAS, the current pressure altitude, and air temperature.

Ground Speed (GS)

Actual speed of the aircraft over the earth surface. Found by correcting true airspeed for wind

CHAPTER 6
FLYING AT NIGHT

CHAPTER 6
Flying At Night

I personally don't think that learners spend enough time flying at night. It wasn't until after I had my private pilot certificate that I spent quality time flying at night and it was intimidating! If you have the opportunity, I suggest flying more than the minimum three hours of required night flying time before earning your Private Pilot Certificate. Go above and beyond and you'll be thankful you did!

Do we use our cones or rods to see at night?

We use our rods to see at night. Rods are estimated to be 10,000 times more sensitive to light than the cones.

Source: PHAK CH 17

What are some methods you can do to protect your night vision?

- Avoid bright lights.
- Dim all GPS screens and flight deck lighting.
- Consider use of oxygen when flying above 5,000 feet.

Source: PHAK CH 17

When are position lights required for night flight?

At all times during night flight.

Source: 14 CFR 91.205

When are anti-collision lights required for night flight?

At all times for aircraft manufactured after August 11, 1971.

Source: 14 CFR 91.205

What color are taxiway lights?

Blue.

What are REILs?

Runway End Identifier Lights.

What color are airport beacons?

White and Green	-	Lighted land airport
Green alone*	-	Lighted land airport
White and Yellow	-	Lighted water airport
Yellow alone*	-	Lighted water airport
Green, Yellow, White	-	Lighted heliport
White, White, Green*	-	Military Airport
White, Green, Red	-	Hospital and/or Emergency Services Heliport

*Green alone or yellow alone is used only in connection with a white-and-green or white-and-yellow beacon display, respectively.

Source: AIM 2-1-9

How do you activate airport lights at night?

Airport lighting is typically controlled by the radio either on unicom or a designated frequency. The frequency can be found in the U.S. Chart Supplement You can control lighting with three intensities.

- Low – Three radio clicks
- Medium – Five radio clicks
- High – Seven radio clicks

Source: AIM 2-1-7

What additional steps should be taken while preflighting at night?

- Be sure you have a flashlight.
- Check all lights including flight deck lighting.
- Take your time!

What procedures should be taken if an engine failure was to occur at night?

Land in a well-lit area, which may mean a road. Avoid dark areas as they may be trees or water. You also want to be near an area, to make getting assistance easier.

What considerations should be taken using anti collision lights at night?

Although not a regulation, it is a courtesy to consider other pilots' night vision. Avoid using anti- collision lights while taxiing, or in proximity to other aircraft operating on or approaching the airport. The bright light can diminish night vision and make flying difficult for fellow pilots.

CHAPTER 7
AIRCRAFT SYSTEMS

CHAPTER 7
Aircraft Systems

This is a subject that can come naturally for some, while others, less mechanically inclined, struggle with it. Knowing your aircraft inside and out can put you at a huge advantage on your checkride, and really boost safety when flying.

What are the four flight control surfaces?

- Ailerons
- Elevator
- Rudder
- Flaps (secondary flight control)

What is the function of the flaps?

Flaps increase lift at slower airspeeds.

How is steering accomplished on the ground?

Pilots use the rudder pedals to control our steerable nose wheel. Note, some airplanes have what is known as a castering nose wheel.

What type of engine is in your aircraft?

This one can be a bit tricky. Although I don't know exactly what airplane you fly, apply the method I share below when describing your airplane. In this case, we're in a Cessna 172M.

This engine is:

A horizontally opposed, aircooled, normal aspirated, direct-drive, Lycoming engine

Let's break down what this means:

- Horizontally opposed – Pistons rest horizontally instead of vertical.
- Air cooled – Air passes over the engine via baffles and cooling fins.
- Normally aspirated – The engine relies on atmospheric pressure for air intake, without a turbocharger.
- Direct Drive – Piston movement turns the crankshaft, which turns the propeller.
- Lycoming – The engine manufacturer.

You could really apply this to any aircraft engine. Talk with your instructor to learn more about your aircraft. You can also contact us at MzeroA support for assistance!
Support@MzeroA.com

What are the four cycles (strokes) of an engine?

- Intake
- Compression
- Power
- Exhaust

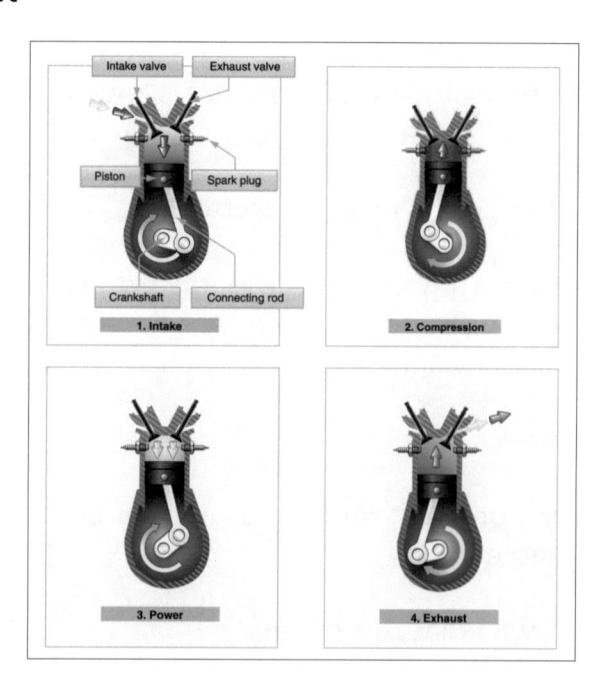

How does the carburetor (carb) heat system work?

Carburetor heat uses unfiltered air from the exhaust manifold to melt ice buildup in the carburetor.

Why does RPM drop when applying carburetor heat?

We are essentially adding heat to the engine, which increases temperature and decreases air density. This causes a decrease in engine performance.

What does the mixture control?

The mixture controls our fuel-to-air ratio (mixture). Generally, done when climbing to higher altitudes, pilots lean the mixture to decrease the amount of fuel. Pilots enrich mixture when descending to lower altitudes where air density is greater.

Explain your airplane's fuel system.

Again, how can I help you with this and not know your aircraft? Well, there are some simple buzzwords that your evaluator is going to want to hear. These include:

The aircraft has ___ gallons of total fuel, and ___ gallons of usable fuel. Making ___ unusable. It has a vented fuel system. The fuel system is gravity-fed, or is driven by an engine-driven fuel pump.

Example: The Cessna 172M has a vented fuel system with 43 gallons of total fuel and 40 gallons of usable fuel making 3 unusable. The system is also powered by an engine driven fuel pump with an electrical fuel pump as a back up.

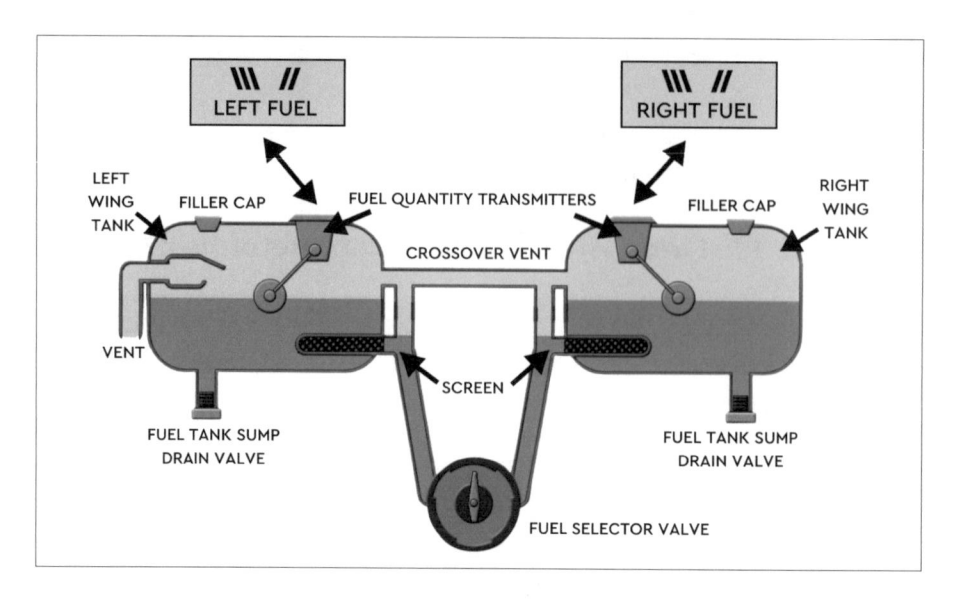

What is the purpose of a fuel pump? Does your aircraft have one?

The fuel pump simply manages continuous fuel flow to the engine. Generally high-wing airplanes use a gravity fed system and therefore don't have a fuel pump.

Explain the electrical system in your aircraft.

This is another question that you may have to look into but again I can give you some "fill in the blank" buzzwords that will really help.

The aircraft has a ___ volt direct current system with a ___ volt battery all driven by a ___ amp alternator.

Example: The Cessna 172M has a 28 volt direct current system with a 24 volt battery all driven by a 60 amp alternator.

Why does the battery have less voltage than the alternator/generator?

The additional voltage of the alternator/generator is used to charge the battery.

What does the electrical system power?

These do not apply to each aircraft, but serve as a rough estimate of what most aircraft electrical systems power. Be sure to review this with your instructor, or go review your AFM/POH and see which apply.

- Lights (beacon, anti-collision, landing light etc.)
- Flaps (This does not apply to every aircraft, for example a Cherokee 140)
- Radios and Avionics
- Interior cabin lighting

What information does the ammeter give?

If the battery is receiving a charge or possibly even an over charge.

What is the purpose of a voltage regulator?

Designed to control aircraft alternator systems. It provides continuous overvoltage protection with warning indication shown through the ammeter.

Which instruments operate on a gyroscope?

- Attitude indicator
- Heading indicator
- Turn coordinator

What are the two main fundamentals of a gyroscope?

Rigidity in space – Based primarily on Newton's first law "A body in motion tends to move at a constant speed and direction unless disturbed by an external force. The spinning gyro inside our instrument maintains a constant attitude as long as no outside force changes it.

Precession – When a deflective force is applied to the rim of a stationary gyro rotor, the rotor moves in the direction of the force. When the rotor is spinning, however, the same force causes the rotor to move in a different direction, as though the force had been applied to a point 90° around the rim in the direction of rotation.

Name the errors that can affect an attitude indicator:

Turn error – During a normal coordinated turn, centrifugal force causes the gyro to precess toward the inside of the turn. This precession increases as the bank increases (steepens). The error disappears as the aircraft rolls out at the end of a 180 degree turn at a normal rollout rate. Therefore, when performing a steep turn, the pilot may use the attitude indicator for rolling in and out of the turn, but use other instruments (VSI and altimeter) during the turn for specific pitch information.

Acceleration error – As the aircraft accelerates (example: during takeoff), there is another type of gyro precession which causes the horizon bar to move down, indicating a slight pitch up attitude. Therefore, takeoffs in low visibility require the use of other instruments such as the altimeter to confirm that a positive rate of climb is established immediately after takeoff.

Deceleration error – Deceleration causes the horizon bar to move up, indicating a false pitch down attitude.

What are some limitations of the heading indicator?

Precession, also sometimes referred to as "drift", is when the heading indicator moves away from the correct heading due to low suction or abrupt maneuvering.

What would the turn coordinator indicate in a slipping/skidding turn?

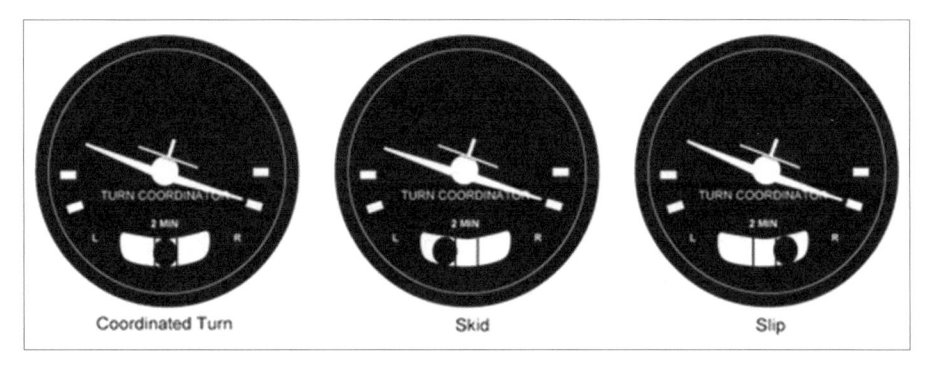

Coordinated Turn — Skid — Slip

Name the compass errors.

Remember *UNOS* and *ANDS*

Turning Errors

- **U** - Undershoot
- **N** - North
- **O** - Overshoot
- **S** - South

Dip Errors

- **A** - Accelerate
- **N** - North
- **D** - Decelerate
- **S** - South

What is the purpose of the alternate static source?

It is used as a backup if the primary static source becomes blocked. Generally, alternate air is not filtered.

If our altimeter was set at 29.20 and we moved it to 30.00 what altitude change would you note?

Altitude would appear to have increased.

How does the pitot static system work?

It operates on the principle of pressure and measures the difference between ram and static pressure. As we climb or descend through the altitudes, the pressure around us is changing. Through the use of aneroid wafers, our instruments in our static system interpret these changes and indicate the proper information.

What instruments operate on the pitot static system?

Airspeed indicator (AI) Vertical speed indicator (VSI) and Altimeter.

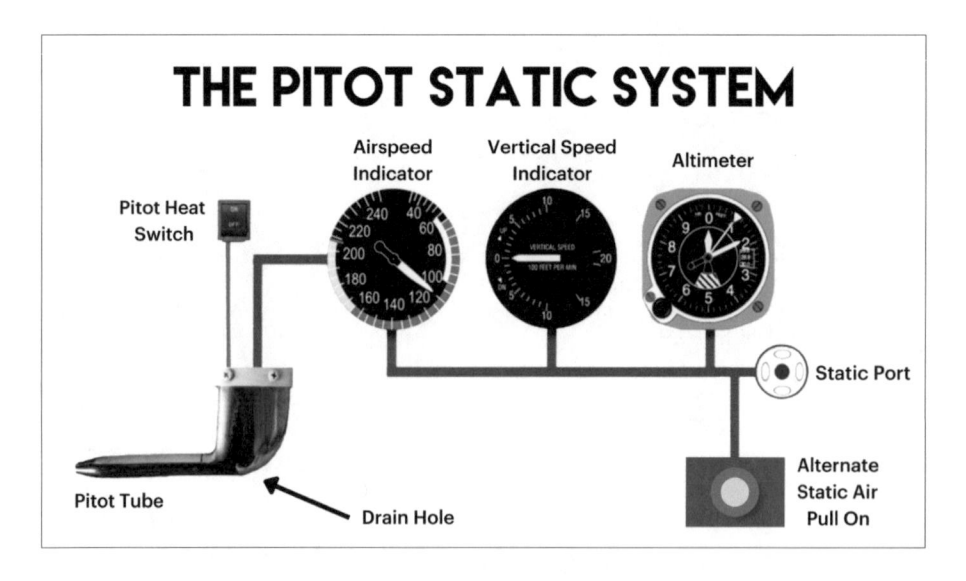

CHAPTER 8
SYSTEM MALFUNCTIONS & EMERGENCY PROCEDURES

CHAPTER 8
System Malfunctions & Emergency Procedures

It's safe to say you will be asked multiple questions on system malfunctions and emergencies on all parts of your checkride including the oral and practical tests. Both your instructor and evaluator must make sure that you, as pilot in command, know how to safely handle these situations.

What is the first indication of carb ice?

Normally, a power reduction. (Please read story below)

Jason's Carb Ice Story:

> I was shooting instrument approaches in the New England area during winter. Approach after approach, we kept going missed because we would reach the altitude minimums without ever seeing the runway. By my fourth attempt, I started getting nervous. It was dark, low IFR conditions, and now it began snowing. Finally, at our minimum altitude my instructor shouts "I SEE THE RUNWAY!" In my excitement I pulled the power back to idle and the engine instantly started sputtering out. "CARB HEAT" was the next thing my instructor shouted. Within seconds of applying it, the engine came back to life. Never again will I forget to turn on carb heat in low engine power settings!!

Define detonation and pre-ignition.

Detonation – Is an uncontrolled firing of the air-fuel mixture within a cylinder usually caused by excessive temperatures. Using lower fuel grades than recommended is a perfect ingredient for causing detonations; this is why we always go a grade up if the recommended fuel grade is unavailable.

Pre-ignition – Occurs when the air-fuel mixture ignites prematurely. Premature burning is usually caused by a residual hotspot in the combustion chamber, often created by a small carbon deposit on a spark plug.

What steps need to be taken if pre-ignition or detonation is detected?

Discontinue the flight, ASAP. Both detonation and pre-ignition can be devastating to engines and can lead to loss of engine power.

What steps should be taken if you get a "bad" RPM drop while checking magnetos?

1. Run up the engine into a higher range (300 to 500 hundred RPMs above normal run-up).
2. Lean the mixture out towards peak EGT.
3. Allow the engine to run at these temperatures for 1 minute.
4. Recheck the fouled side.

What does low oil pressure mean and what should you do about it?

Low oil pressure is never a good sign for engine performance. There is an issue with the oil system, potentially an oil leak, and you should land the airplane as soon as practicable. Pick the closest airport and proceed to it immediately.

What procedures should you take following a partial loss of power?

A partial loss of power should be treated just like a complete loss of power because a complete loss of power is likely to follow (See below).

What procedures should you take following a complete loss of power?

A complete or partial loss of power is a scary situation. To help us remain calm in this situation, we teach the ABCs of an engine failure:

A – Airspeed – Establish your airplane's best glide speed. We want to stay aloft as long as possible.

B – Best Landing Area – Pick out your best landing area, keeping in mind it may be behind you or below you so don't get tunnel vision! Be sure to stay committed to that landing site once selected.

C – Checklist – Consult your emergency checklist if you have time. Consider learning a "flow check" that way you have your emergency checklist memorized.

What procedures should you conduct following an engine fire in flight?

Always use your airplane's AFM for recommended procedures. However, the general procedure for an engine fire in flight is:

1. Mixture – Cutoff
2. Fuel Shutoff Valve – Off
3. Master Switch – Off
4. Cabin Air/Heat – Off
5. Airspeed – Emergency Descent

What procedures should you take following an engine fire on the ground?

If the engine does not start – Continue cranking to suck flames back into the engine. Evacuate and extinguish.

If the engine does start – Allow the engine to run for about a minute, shut down, and inspect damage.

Note: Cold weather starts are prime candidates for engine fires during start.

What is the minimum altitude you can descend to while conducting a simulated emergency approach?

This question is huge! So please take note. Some learners fail their checkride on this common flight procedure because their instructors never told them!

The minimum safe altitude over a non-congested area is **500 feet AGL**; you cannot descend below that! So while conducting your simulated emergency procedure on your checkride, pretend that 500 feet AGL is the ground. I recommend my learners to go around at 600 feet AGL just to be safe and not bust the altitude regulation.

What is CFIT?

CFIT stands for Controlled Flight Into Terrain. Its best definition is flying a perfectly good airplane into terrain. This can be caused by low visibility and/or poor situational awareness.

What would you do if the engine began running rough in-flight?

The obvious answer here that EVERY evaluator wants to hear is to land ASAP. This isn't quite meant for an off-airport landing, but you should have a good idea of a field just in case.

Explain to the evaluator in a similar way: "I'm going to find the nearest airport and start to head toward it. However, I'm always going to have a way out (an open field etc.) assuming the engine conditions worsen."

Don't forget to troubleshoot and run through your emergency procedures checklist. (mixture rich, fuel selector on etc...)

How long will your battery last in the event of an alternator failure?

A typical battery may last approximately 15 – 30 minutes. Don't count on it for longer than that while in flight.

What will you lose if you lose the battery?

Anything electronic: GPS, radios, flaps (in some aircraft) etc...

Keep in mind the engine will still be running. However, to conserve the battery, it's recommended to turn off all unnecessary electronics.

If your vacuum system failed, which two instruments would you lose?

Attitude Indicator and Heading Indicator

CHAPTER 9
AIRSPACE

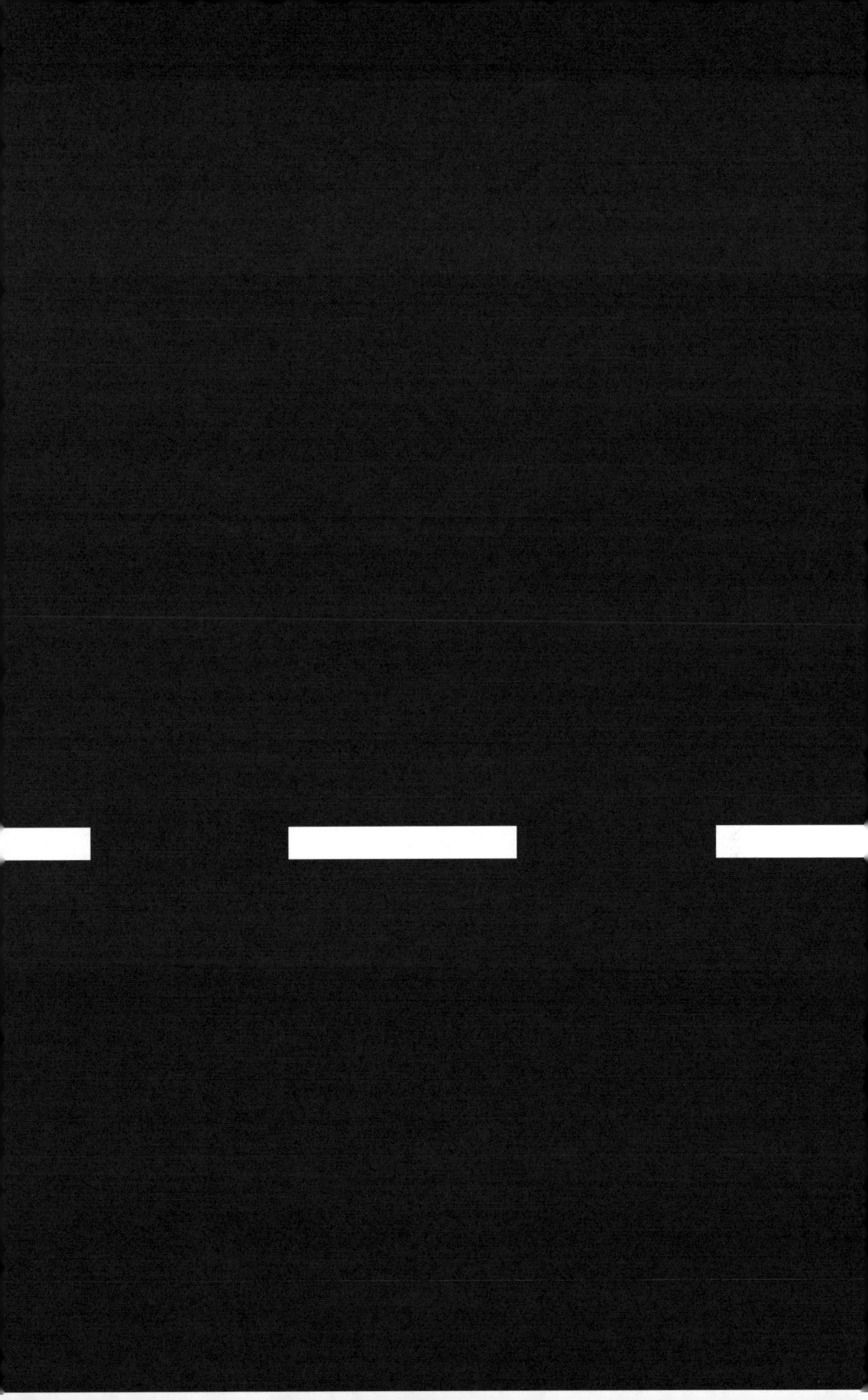

CHAPTER 9
Airspace

Many learners don't get enough "real-world" flying. Some instructors are reluctant to give Class B airspace endorsements, or send their learners to busier airports. The following questions give you the full breakdown on each type of airspace so you'll be checkride and real-world ready.

What is Class A airspace?

Class A airspace is not shown on your sectional. It exists from 18,000 feet MSL up to and including FL600.

What are the VFR cloud clearance requirements in Class A airspace?

This is a trick question evaluators like to ask, don't fall for it. All pilots must be on an IFR flight plan in Class A airspace. There are no VFR cloud clearance requirements.

What is Class B airspace?

Class B airspace surrounds the nation's busiest airports and usually goes as high as 10,000 feet MSL, in some cases, even higher. The uppermost level of Class B airspace may extend horizontally, with a radius of up to 15 nautical miles around the airport tower. There is, however, no universal set of Class B dimensions since the flow of traffic, geography, and other considerations determine the exact architecture of each Class B area. A sectional or VFR Terminal Area Chart is very helpful in understanding the design and lateral dimensions of each Class B airspace.

How is Class B depicted on a sectional chart?

Class B is shown by solid blue lines.

As a student pilot, can you fly solo into Class B airspace?

Yes, but only with a proper endorsement from your instructor for that specific B airspace. Note that some Class B airports prohibit student pilots.

Is a Mode C transponder required in B airspace?

Yes, in fact, you even need a Mode C transponder (altitude encoding) within the class B Mode C Veil.

Do you have to communicate with ATC in Class B airspace?

Yes, two-way radio communications with controlling ATC are required. You must also hear those magic words "Cleared into Class Bravo Airspace".

What are the VFR visibility and cloud clearance requirements in Class B airspace?

3 statute miles visibility, and remain clear of clouds.

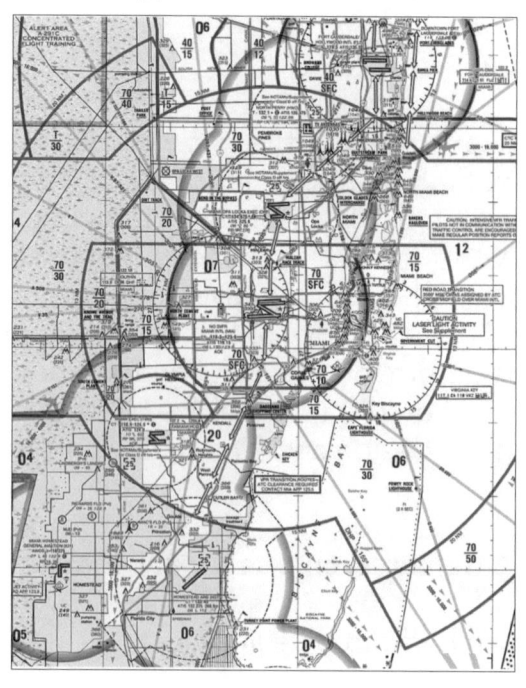

tWhat is Class C airspace?

Class C airports are not quite as big as Class B airports, and differ quite a bit in requirements.

How is Class C depicted on a sectional?

By solid magenta lines.

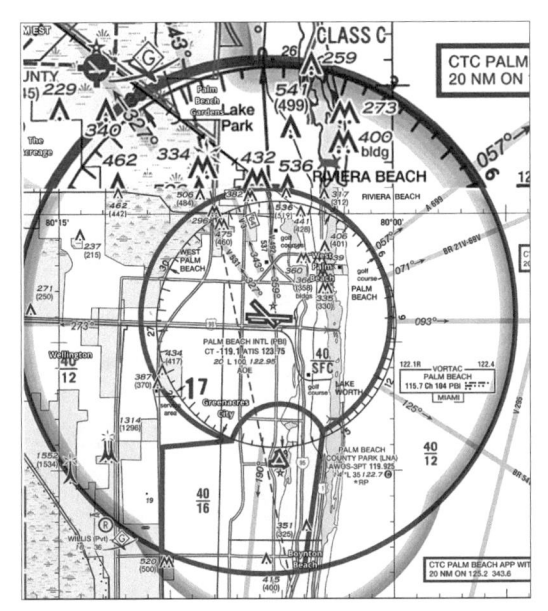

As a student pilot, can you fly solo into Class C airspace?

Yes, you can fly into Class C as a student pilot.

Is a Mode C transponder required in Class C airspace?

Yes.

Do you have to communicate with ATC in Class C airspace?

Yes, two-way radio communications are required.

What are the VFR visibility and cloud clearance requirements in Class C airspace?

3 statute miles visibility, and 1,000 feet above the clouds, 500 feet below the clouds, and 2,000 feet horizontal from the clouds. (Easily remembered by using 3-152)

What is Class D airspace?

Class D airports tend to be relatively small, but that doesn't mean they're not busy. I've sat many times simply waiting for a takeoff clearance at a Class D airport because it was so busy. Class D airspace reverts to Class E or G airspace when the ATC tower is not operating. Check the Chart Supplement for each specific airport information.

How is Class D depicted on a sectional?

By dashed blue lines.

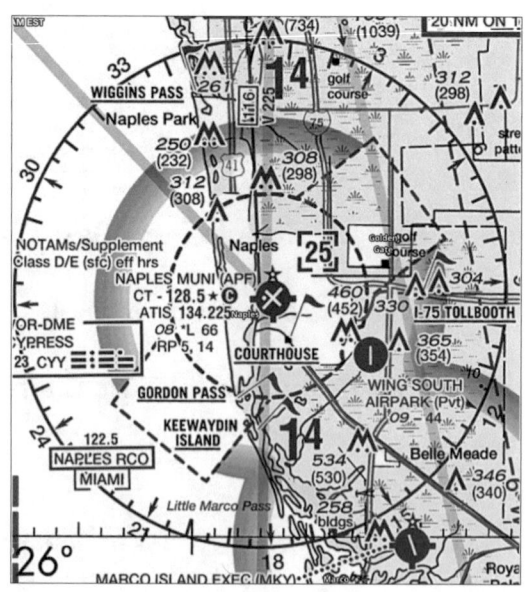

As a student pilot, can you fly solo into Class D airspace?

Yes.

Is a Mode C transponder required in Class D airspace?

No.

Do you have to communicate with ATC in Class D airspace?

Yes, two-way radio communications are required.

What are the VFR visibility and cloud clearance requirements in Class D airspace?

3 statute miles visibility, and 1,000 feet above the clouds, 500 feet below the clouds, and 2,000 feet horizontal from the clouds. (Easily remembered by 3–152)

What is Class E airspace?

Class E airspace can be tough to understand; it can start anywhere from the surface to 14,500 feet MSL. It is charted differently, depending on what altitude it begins on the sectional. You may have to read this section a few times to fully understand it.

Is Class E airspace controlled?

Yes, Class E airspace is controlled, but unlike A, B, C, and D airspace, pilots do not have to communicate with ATC when in it unless on a flight plan.

What are the VFR visibility and cloud clearance requirements in Class E airspace?

3 statute miles, and 1,000 ft above the clouds, 500 ft below the clouds, and 2,000 ft horizontal from the clouds. (Remember that by saying 3–152)

However, above 10,000 feet, the requirements are 5 statute miles visibility, 1,000 feet above the clouds, 1,000 feet below the clouds, and 1 mile horizontally from the clouds.

What are the different types of Class E airspace?

Use the acronym **SETVODA**:

- **S** - **Surface** - Class E starting on the surface depicted by dashed magenta lines.

- **E** - **Extension** – A Class E surface extension usually to protect an instrument approach also depicted by dashed magenta lines.

- **T** - **Transition** – Area to show Class E that starts at 700 feet AGL depicted by shaded magenta lines.

- **V** - **Victor Airway** – Victor airways are Class E airspace.

- **O** - **Offshore** – shown on sectional varies with area. Depicted by a blue zipper line. Altitude is usually listed inside the zipper line area and charted in MSL.

- **D** - **Domestic Enroute** – Most areas where Class E does not start at the surface or 700 feet AGL. Domestic Enroute E starts at 1,200 feet AGL.

- **A** - **Above 14,500 MSL-** When not depicted otherwise, Class E starts at 14,500 feet MSL, and extends up to but does not include 18,000 feet MSL.

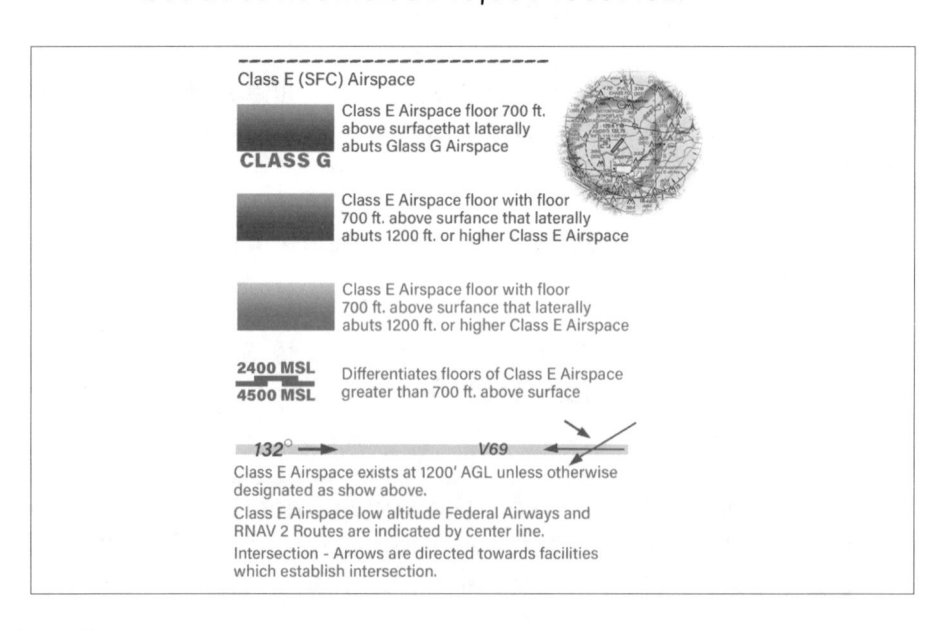

Class E (SFC) Airspace

CLASS G — Class E Airspace floor 700 ft. above surface that laterally abuts Glass G Airspace

Class E Airspace floor with floor 700 ft. above surface that laterally abuts 1200 ft. or higher Class E Airspace

Class E Airspace floor with floor 700 ft. above surface that laterally abuts 1200 ft. or higher Class E Airspace

2400 MSL / 4500 MSL — Differentiates floors of Class E Airspace greater than 700 ft. above surface

132° → V69 ← Class E Airspace exists at 1200' AGL unless otherwise designated as show above.

Class E Airspace low altitude Federal Airways and RNAV 2 Routes are indicated by center line.

Intersection - Arrows are directed towards facilities which establish intersection.

What is Class G airspace?

Class G airspace is the airspace not designated as A,B,C,D or E. Class G airspace is uncontrolled.

What are the VFR visibility and cloud clearance requirements in Class G airspace?

Day: 1 mile visibility and clear of clouds.

Night: 3 statute miles, and 1,000 feet above the clouds, 500 feet below the clouds, and 2,000 feet horizontal from the clouds. (Easily remembered by using 3-152)

When Flying at 1,200 ft AGL and below –

Day: 1 mile visibility and clear of clouds.

Night: 3 miles visibility, maintain 1,000 ft. above, 500 ft. below, 2,000 ft. horizontally from the clouds.

What is ADS-B?

ADS-B stands for Automatic Dependent Surveillance-Broadcast. It is the preferred method of satellite based surveillance for ATC in the National Airspace System.

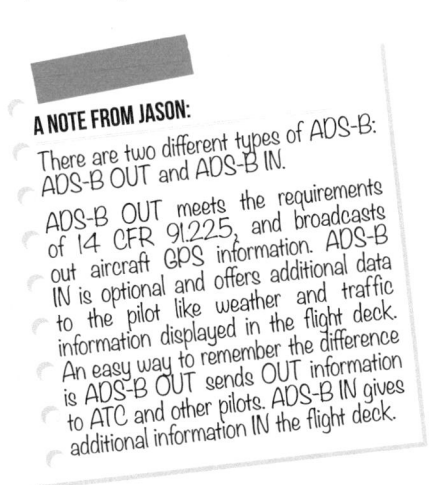

> **A NOTE FROM JASON:**
> There are two different types of ADS-B: ADS-B OUT and ADS-B IN.
>
> ADS-B OUT meets the requirements of 14 CFR 91.225, and broadcasts out aircraft GPS information. ADS-B IN is optional and offers additional data to the pilot like weather and traffic information displayed in the flight deck. An easy way to remember the difference is ADS-B OUT sends OUT information to ATC and other pilots. ADS-B IN gives additional information IN the flight deck.

When is ADS-B required?

- Class A, B, and C airspace.
- Within 30 nautical miles of the Mode C veil of a Class B primary airport.
- Class E airspace at or above 10,000 feet MSL, excluding airspace at and below 2,500 feet AGL.
- Above the ceiling and within the lateral boundaries of Class B or Class C airspace up to 10,000 feet. ADS-B is not required below a Class B or Class C airspace shelf if it is outside of a Mode C veil.
- Class E airspace over the Gulf of Mexico, at and above 3,000 feet MSL when within 12 NM of the U.S. coast.

Source: 14 CFR 91.225

AIRSPACE FEATURES: CLASS A

Operations Permitted: **IFR**
Entry Requirements: **ATC Clearance**
Minimum Pilot Qualifications:
Instrument Rating
Two-Way Radio Communications
Required: **Yes**
Minimum VFR Visibility
(below 10,000 MSL): **N/A**
Minimum Distance From Clouds (below 10,000 MSL): **N/A**
Minimum Distance From Clouds (above 10,000 MSL): **N/A**
Aircraft Separation: **All Aircraft**
Traffic Advisories: **Yes**

AIRSPACE FEATURES: CLASS B

Operations Permitted: **VFR & IFR**
Entry Requirements: **ATC Clearance**
Minimum Pilot Qualifications: **Private Pilot Certificate / Student Pilot**
Two-Way Radio Communications
Required: **Yes**
Minimum VFR Visibility
(below 10,000 MSL): **3 Statue Miles**
Minimum Distance From Clouds (below 10,000 MSL): **Clear of Clouds**
Minimum Distance From Clouds (above 10,000 MSL): **Clear of Clouds**
Aircraft Separation: **All Aircraft**
Traffic Advisories: **Yes**

AIRSPACE FEATURES: CLASS C

Operations Permitted: **VFR & IFR**
Entry Requirements: **IFR: Clearance; VFR: Radio Contact**
Minimum Pilot Qualifications:
Student Pilot
Two-Way Radio Communications
Required: **Yes**
Minimum VFR Visibility
(below 10,000 MSL): **3 Statue Miles**
Minimum Distance From Clouds (below 10,000 MSL): **1,000 Above 500 Below 2,000 Horizontally**
Minimum Distance From Clouds (above 10,000 MSL): **1,000 Above 500 Below 2,000 Horizontally**
Aircraft Separation: **IFR, Special VFR and Runway Operations**
Traffic Advisories: **Yes**

AIRSPACE FEATURES: CLASS D

Operations Permitted: **VFR & IFR**
Entry Requirements: **IFR: Clearance; VFR: Radio Contact**
Minimum Pilot Qualifications:
Student Pilot
Two-Way Radio Communications
Required: **Yes**
Minimum VFR Visibility
(below 10,000 MSL): **3 Statue Miles**
Minimum Distance From Clouds (below 10,000 MSL): **1,000 Above 500 Below 2,000 Horizontally**
Minimum Distance From Clouds (above 10,000 MSL): **1,000 Above 500 Below 2,000 Horizontally**
Aircraft Separation: **IFR, Special VFR and Runway Operations**
Traffic Advisories: **Workload Permitting**

AIRSPACE FEATURES: CLASS E

Operations Permitted: **VFR & IFR**
Entry Requirements: **IFR: Clearance; VFR: None**
Minimum Pilot Qualifications:
Student Pilot
Two-Way Radio Communications
Required: **IFR Only**
Minimum VFR Visibility
(below 10,000 MSL): **3 Statue Miles**
Minimum Distance From Clouds (below 10,000 MSL): **1,000 Above 500 Below 2,000 Horizontally**
Minimum Distance From Clouds (above 10,000 MSL): **1,000 Above 1,000 Below 1 Mile Horizontally**
Aircraft Separation: **IFR, Special VFR**
Traffic Advisories: **Workload Permitting**

AIRSPACE FEATURES: CLASS G

Operations Permitted: **VFR & IFR**
Entry Requirements: **None**
Minimum Pilot Qualifications:
Student Pilot
Two-Way Radio Communications
Required: **No**
Minimum VFR Visibility
(below 10,000 MSL): **Day – 1 Statue Mile; Night – 3 Statue Miles**
Minimum Distance From Clouds (below 10,000 MSL):
Clear of Clouds**
Minimum Distance From Clouds (above 10,000 MSL): **1,000 Above 500 Below 2,000 Horizontally****
Aircraft Separation: **None**
Traffic Advisories: **Workload Permitting**

Name and define the different types of special use airspace.

For this we have the acronym MCPRAWN (Mc – Prawn):

- M - Military Operations Area (MOA)
- C - Controlled Firing Area
- P - Prohibited Area
- R - Restricted Area
- A - Alert Area
- W - Warning Area
- N - National Security (TFR)

Military Operations Area (MOA)

These large areas of the country are shown on your sectional as enclosed by a line of magenta hash marks with a sharp outer edge. Military operations such as training exercises come and go. Permission to fly in an MOA is not required. Caution should be used when operating in a MOA.

Controlled Firing Area

Here there may be military activity such as artillery fire that is suspended when radar detects approaching aircraft. Thus, these Controlled Firing Areas are not shown on the sectional.

Prohibited Area

A prohibited area, shown and clearly marked with the words "Prohibited" on your sectional, is an area enclosed in a unique wide blue border with a sharp outer edge. No civil aircraft can enter a prohibited area.

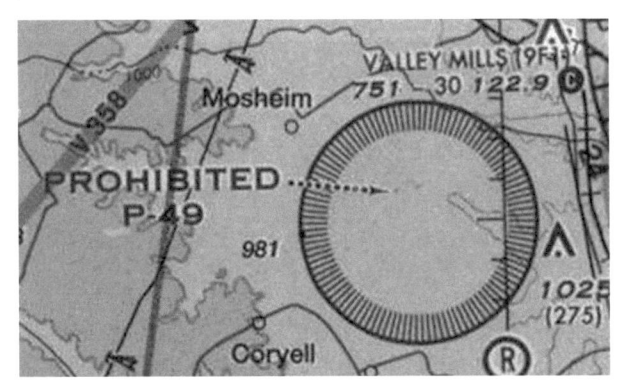

Restricted Area

A restricted area may be quite large and is shown on the sectional with a wide blue line of hash marks and a sharp outer edge. The image shows several Restricted Areas of various shapes all pieced together. Unseen hazards such as artillery practice, missile firing and other activities may take place. Travel in a Restricted Area may be possible when it is not activated, but permission MUST be obtained by the controlling agency. Your sectional has a table that gives the floor and ceiling of Restricted Areas as well as the times of use and the controlling agency.

Alert Area

An alert area is depicted similar to a Restricted and Prohibited area, but the identifier is an A. We are allowed to fly into Alert Areas without prior permission. An Alert Area may involve high general aviation traffic, unusual air operations or frequent pilot training. The area will be marked with a blue border with a word or two of explanation.

Warning Area

This is a hazardous area that lies over international waters, beyond the three mile coastal limit.

National Security TFR

TFR stands for temporary flight restriction. These can be found around sporting events, presidential events etc. They are No-Fly zones.

Which Airspace falls under the "Other Airspace" category?

- TRSAs (Terminal Radar Service Area)
- Military Training Routes
- Wildlife Refuge Areas

CHAPTER 10
THE NATIONAL TRANSPORTATION SAFETY BOARD (NTSB)

CHAPTER 10
The National Transportation Safety Board (NTSB)

National Transportation Safety Board (NTSB) information is very dry, but is important information. We do our best to break down the information and present it in an easy to follow manner.

Define an aircraft accident.

An occurrence associated with the operation of an aircraft which takes place between the time any person boards the aircraft with the intention of flight and all such persons have disembarked, and in which any person suffers death or serious injury, or in which the aircraft receives substantial damage.

Define an aircraft incident.

An occurrence other than an accident, associated with the operation of an aircraft, which affects or could affect the safety of operations.

When is immediate notification of the NTSB required?

When an aircraft accident or any of the following listed incidents occur:

- Flight control system malfunction or failure.
- Inability of any required flight crew member to perform normal flight duties as a result of injury or illness.
- In-flight fire.
- Aircraft collision in flight.
- Damage to property, other than the aircraft, estimated to exceed $25,000 for repair (including materials and labor), or fair market value in the event of total loss, whichever is less.

What is the NTSB definition of a serious injury?

An injury which:

- Requires hospitalization for more than 48 hours, starting within 7 days of the injury was received.
- Fracture of any bone (except simple fractures of fingers, toes, or nose).
- Injury causes severe hemorrhages (severe bleeding), nerve, muscle or tendon damage.
- Involves any internal organ.
- Or, involves second or third-degree burns affecting more than 5% of the body surface.

SOLVE THE SCENARIO

Consider the following:

You're the captain of a large airliner. Before you start to taxi, the flight attendant trips and spills a pot of coffee on a passenger who receives a second degree burn.

Is this an accident or incident?

This is an accident because the person boarded the airplane with the intent to fly and sustained a serious injury.

Why is this a serious injury?

Because the passenger sustained a second-degree burn.

When should you file a report with the NTSB?

When requested by the NTSB, you must file your report within ten days.

Source: 49 CFR Part 830

CHAPTER 11
FAR/AIM

CHAPTER 11
FAR/AIM

The FAR/AIM can be daunting due to its length and complex legal language. This review chapter will only cover what you need to know for your private pilot certificate. We'll keep it simple for you to manage! Don't forget that the AIM is a excellent source of information for best practices and is essential for understanding the regulations clearly. It explains regulations in plain English and numerous helpful figures and diagrams.

What are the FAA's restrictions on alcohol consumption for pilots?

No person may act or attempt to act as a crewmember of a civil aircraft within 8 hours after the consumption of any alcoholic beverage, under the influence of alcohol, or when having a blood alcohol level of .04 or greater.

Source: 14 CFR 91.17

Under what conditions is it permissible to drop objects from an airplane?

No pilot in command of a civil aircraft may allow any object to be dropped from that aircraft in flight if it creates a hazard to persons or property. However, this section does not prohibit the dropping of any object if reasonable precautions are taken to avoid injury or damage to persons or property.

Source: 14 CFR 91.15

What specific preflight action are required before every flight?

Before each flight, the pilot in command must review all pertinent information including:

- For a flight not in the vicinity of an airport, weather reports and forecasts, fuel requirements, alternatives

available if the planned flight cannot be completed, and any known traffic delays of which the pilot in command has been advised by ATC.
- For any flight, runway lengths at airports of intended use, and the following takeoff and landing distance information.
- For civil aircraft for which an approved Airplane or Rotorcraft Flight Manual containing takeoff and landing distance data is required, the takeoff and landing distance data contained therein; and other reliable information appropriate to the aircraft, relating to aircraft performance under expected values of airport elevation and runway slope, aircraft gross weight, and wind and temperature.

Source: 14 CFR 91.103

When must seat belts and shoulder harnesses mandatory in an airplane?

No pilot may take off a U.S.-registered civil aircraft unless the pilot in command of that aircraft ensures that each person on board is briefed on how to fasten and unfasten that person's safety belt and, if installed, shoulder harness.

All passengers and crew must be secured with seat belts during taxi, takeoff, and landing.

Pilots must keep the safety belt fastened while at the crewmember station unless necessary to perform needed duties. If shoulder harnesses are installed, pilots must wear shoulder harnesses during takeoff and landing unless unable to perform needed duties.

Source: 14 CFR 91.107

What are the right-of-way rules?

Pilots must maintain vigilance to see and avoid other aircraft regardless of whether the operation is under IFR or VFR. Pilots must yield to aircraft with right-of-way and avoid passing over, under, or ahead unless well clear.

In distress

An aircraft in distress has the right-of-way over all other air traffic.

Converging

When aircraft of the same category are converging at approximately the same altitude (except head-on, or nearly so), the aircraft to the other's right has the right-of-way. For different categories of aircraft:

- A balloon has the right-of-way over any other category of aircraft.
- A glider has the right-of-way over an airship, powered parachute, weight-shift-control aircraft, airplane, or rotorcraft.
- An airship has the right-of-way over a powered parachute, weight-shift-control aircraft, airplane, or rotorcraft.
- However, an aircraft towing or refueling other aircraft has the right-of-way over all other engine-driven aircraft.

Approaching head-on

When aircraft are approaching each other head-on, or nearly so, each pilot of each aircraft shall alter course to the right.

Overtaking

The aircraft being overtaken has right-of-way; overtaking aircraft must pass to the right.

Landing

Aircraft, while on final approach to land or while landing, have the right-of-way over other aircraft in flight or operating on the surface, except that they shall not take advantage of this rule to force an aircraft off the runway surface which has already landed and is attempting to make way for an aircraft on final approach. When two or more aircraft are approaching an airport for the purpose of landing, the aircraft at the lower altitude has the right-of-way, but it shall not take advantage of this rule to cut in front of another which is on final approach to land or to overtake that aircraft.

Source: 14 CFR 91.113

What is the minimum safe altitude to operate an aircraft over a congested area?

Over any congested area of a city, town, or settlement, or over any open air assembly of persons, an altitude of 1,000 feet above the highest obstacle within a horizontal radius of 2,000 feet of the aircraft.

Source: 14 CFR 91.119

What are the rules about areas categorized as other than "congested?"

An altitude of 500 feet above the surface, except over open water or sparsely populated areas. In those cases, the aircraft may not be operated closer than 500 feet to any person, vessel, vehicle, or structure.

Source: 14 CFR 91.119

Explain the light gun signals.

Keep a copy of this chart with you in your flight bag for reference if you ever need it.

ATC Light Gun Signals

Color	On Ground	In Flight
Steady Green	Cleared For Takeoff	Cleared To Land
Flashing Green	Cleared To Taxi	Return To Land
Steady Red	Stop	Give Way To Other Aircraft
Flashing Red	Taxi Clear of Runway	Airport Unsafe - Do Not Land
Flashing White	Return To Starting Point on Airport	N/A
Alternating Red and Green	Exercise Extreme Caution	Exercise Extreme Caution

What procedures should be taken to receive light gun signals?

Squawk 7600, enter the traffic pattern as prescribed (45-degree entry to left downwind), and watch tower for light gun signals.

What instruments are required for VFR day? VFR night?

To help us remember this, we use the acronym **A TOMATO FLAMES**. For night operations, we add **FLAPS** to that acronym.

- **A** - Airspeed Indicator

- **T** - Tachometer
- **O** - Oil Pressure
- **M** - Manifold Pressure
- **A** - Altimeter
- **T** - Temperature gauge
- **O** - Oil Temperature

- **F** - Fuel Level
- **L** - Landing Gear Indicator
- **A** - Anti-collision Lights
- **M** - Magnetic Heading Indicator
- **E** - Emergency Locator Transmitter (ELT)
- **S** - Seat Belts

Note: A common question I usually get from my learners is, "We don't have a manifold pressure gauge or a landing gear position indicator. How can we still fly and not break the regs?"

If our aircraft is not equipped for such items like a fixed gear or normally aspirated engine, then the manifold gauge and gear indicator would not be required.

VFR Night Requirements

Requirements for VFR Night flight can be found in 91.205c. They include the items in **A TOMATO FLAMES** and **FLAPS.**

F - Fuses (not required if airplane uses circuit breakers)
L - Landing lights (if operating for hire)
A - Anticollision lights
P - Position indicator lights
S - Source of power

This part can get a bit confusing. Again, only if your aircraft is equipped would you need the item. For example, if your airplane has circuit breakers, you would not need to have fuses.

Notice that anti-collision lights have come up twice: once for day and once for night. It's the dates that come into play here. For day flight, if your aircraft was registered after March 11th, 1996, they would be required all the time. For night flights, they are required for all aircraft registered after August 11th, 1971. So my little 1975 150M would be required to have anti-collision lights for night flight, but not for day.

Source: 14 CFR 91.205

What are the fuel requirements for VFR day? VFR night?

No person may begin a flight in an airplane under VFR conditions unless (considering wind and forecast weather conditions) there is enough fuel to fly to the first point of intended landing and, assuming normal cruising speed:

During the day, to fly after that for at least 30 minutes; or
At night, to fly after that for at least 45 minutes.

Source: 14 CFR 91.151

What is an ELT?

ELT stands for Emergency Locator Transmitter. It's the device used to help locate the airplane in the event it goes missing.

NOTE: There are two types of ELTs. The new 406 MHZ ELT which is more accurate and is now the industry standard and the older 121.5 MHz ELT which many pilots still have but are now considered obsolete.

When is an ELT NOT required?

- Aircraft while engaged in scheduled flights by scheduled air carriers.
- Aircraft while engaged in training operations conducted entirely within a 50-nautical mile radius of the airport from which such local flight operations began.
- Aircraft while engaged in flight operations incident to the aerial application of chemicals and other substances for agricultural purposes.
- Aircraft equipped to carry not more than one person.

Source: 14 CFR 91.207

What are the requirements regarding the use of supplemental oxygen?

- Above 12,500 ft MSL to and including 14,000 ft MSL – Crew only must use oxygen at these altitudes for portions of flight at those altitudes that are greater than 30 minutes.
- Above 14,000 ft MSL – Crew must use oxygen at all times at these altitudes.
- Above 15,000 ft MSL- Passengers must be provided oxygen but are not required to use it.

Source: 14 CFR 91.211

What is a VASI?

VASI stands for Visual Approach Slope Indicator. It's a lighting system typically to the left of a runway used to help you maintain a safe glide-path on landing. VASI gives visual descent guidance for landing.

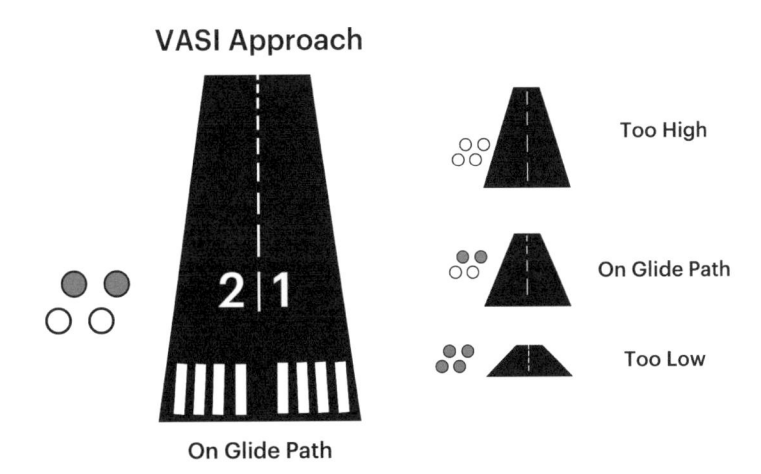

VASI Approach

What is a PAPI?

PAPI stands for Precision Approach Path Indicator. It's a lighting system typically to the left of a runway used to help you maintain a safe glide path on landing.

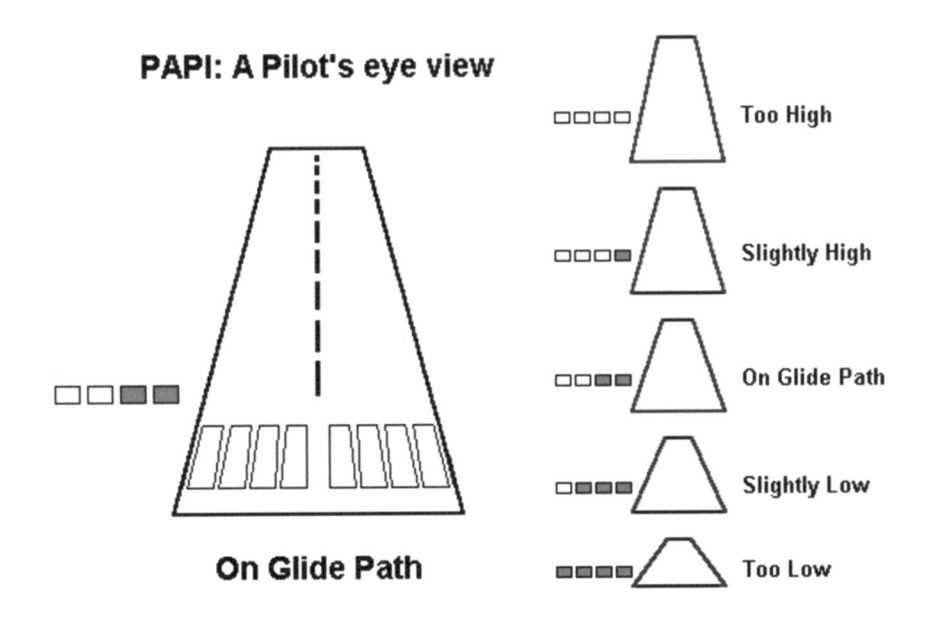

Be able to define the following airport lighting aids:

- Airport beacon
- Taxiway lights
- Runway lights
- VASI or PAPI
- Threshold Lights
- Runway end identifier lights (REIL)

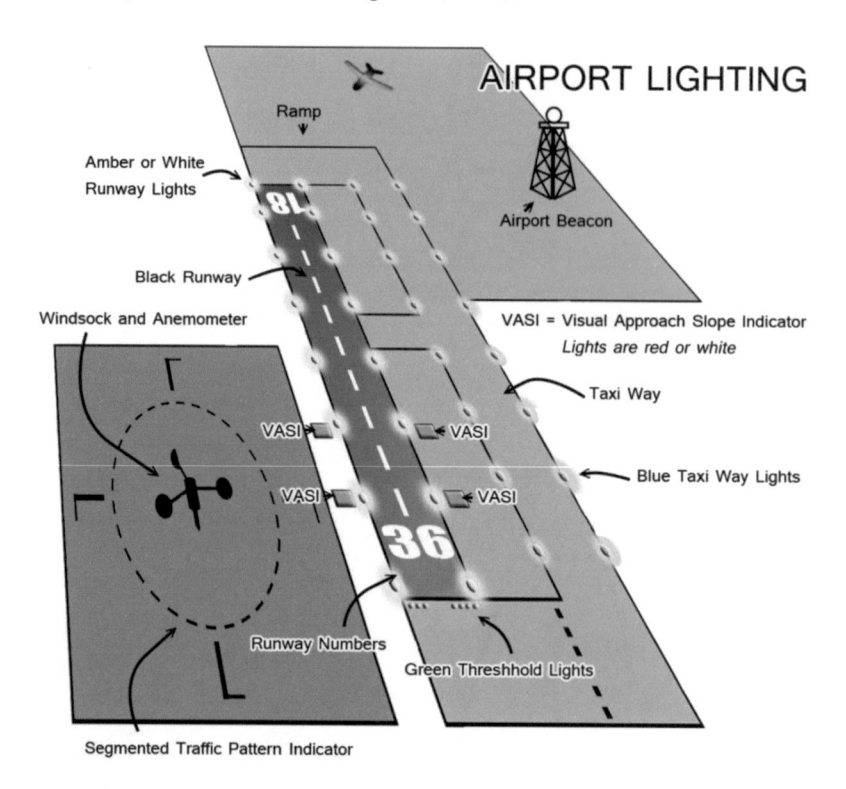

Be able to define these runway markings:

- Threshold markings
- Designation marking
- Aiming point (touchdown zone)

What is standard altitude for a traffic pattern?

Typically field elevation plus 1,000 feet with rounding to the nearest hundred feet to make it easier. For example: Field elevation at my home airport is 80 feet so we'll fly our patterns at 1,100 feet because we round that 80 to 100. Flying at exactly 1,080 feet would just be tough.

What direction are turns in a standard traffic pattern?

Left, unless otherwise noted in the Chart Supplement U.S.

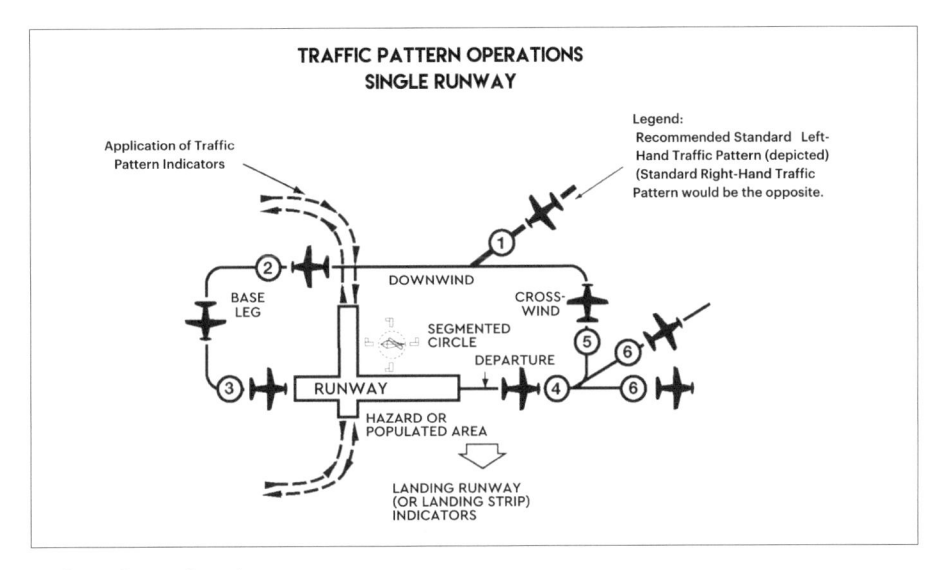

What is Zulu time?

Ok, this one ranks right up there on a top ten list of most confusing things to explain. Don't get discouraged.

Zulu Time is the world time. It is also known as UTC (Universal Time Coordinated). Zulu time is the same all over the world and helps cut down on confusion.

The thing that makes it so confusing is daylight saving time. The way we convert to Zulu changes often because of daylight saving time.

To make the conversion from your local time, find the time in the first column labeled "Local." If you are on Eastern Daylight Saving Time (EDT), you would use the second column to find your Zulu time/UTC. For instance, if it's 11 a.m. Eastern Daylight Saving Time in Washington, D.C., it's 1500 hours in Zulu time.

LOCAL	EDT	EST	CDT	CST	MDT	MST	PDT	PST
Midnight	0400	0500	0500	0600	0600	0700	0700	0800
1 a.m.	0500	0600	0600	0700	0700	0800	0800	0900
2 a.m.	0600	0700	0700	0800	0800	0900	0900	1000
3 a.m.	0700	0800	0800	0900	0900	1000	1000	1100
4 a.m.	0800	0900	0900	1000	1000	1100	1100	1200
5 a.m.	0900	1000	1000	1100	1100	1200	1200	1300
6 a.m.	1000	1100	1100	1200	1200	1300	1300	1400
7 a.m.	1100	1200	1200	1300	1300	1400	1400	1500
8 a.m.	1200	1300	1300	1400	1400	1500	1500	1600
9 a.m.	1300	1400	1400	1500	1500	1600	1600	1700
10 a.m.	1400	1500	1500	1600	1600	1700	1700	1800
11 a.m.	1500	1600	1600	1700	1700	1800	1800	1900
NOON	1600	1700	1700	1800	1800	1900	1900	2000
1 p.m.	1700	1800	1800	1900	1900	2000	2000	2100
2 p.m.	1800	1900	1900	2000	2000	2100	2100	2200
3 p.m.	1900	2000	2000	2100	2100	2200	2200	2300
4 p.m.	2000	2100	2100	2200	2200	2300	2300	2400
5 p.m.	2100	2200	2200	2300	2300	2400	2400	0100
6 p.m.	2200	2300	2300	2400	2400	0100	0100	0200
7 p.m.	2300	2400	2400	0100	0100	0200	0200	0300
8 p.m.	2400	0100	0100	0200	0200	0300	0300	0400
9 p.m.	0100	0200	0200	0300	0300	0400	0400	0500
10 p.m.	0200	0300	0300	0400	0400	0500	0500	0600
11 p.m.	0300	0400	0400	0500	0500	0600	0600	0700
LOCAL	EDT	EST	CDT	CST	MDT	MST	PDT	PST

LEGEND:
EDT = Eastern Daylight Saving Time
EST = Eastern Standard Time
CDT = Central Daylight Saving Time
CST = Central Standard Time
MDT = Mountain Daylight Saving Time
MST = Mountain Standard Time
PDT = Pacific Daylight Saving Time
PST = Pacific Standard Time

What is wake turbulence?

Also known as "wing tip vortices," wake turbulence is a by-product of lift created by all aircraft but essentially more threatening from large airplanes.

How can you avoid wake turbulence?

On Takeoff

Rotate before the preceding aircraft's point of rotation and stay above that aircrafts glide path, or upwind of it.

On Landing

Stay above that aircraft's glide path and land beyond that aircraft's touchdown point.

What does the term LAHSO mean?

Land and Hold Short Operations. LAHSO operations require an aircraft to land and hold short of another runway or taxiway.

What items must a pilot brief passengers on before departure?

- No smoking
- Use of safety belts and shoulder harnesses
- Location of exits
- Location of survival equipment
- Normal emergency procedures

Source: 14 CFR 91.519

What is meant by the term line up and wait?

Line up and wait is somewhat new to American aviation phraseology but has been in use with international pilots for some time. It has taken the place of the phrase Position and Hold which means the same thing. The FAA adopted the international standard terminology to avoid confusion.

CHAPTER 12
CROSS COUNTRY FLIGHT PLANNING

CHAPTER 12
Cross Country Flight Planning

We are now at the last chapter and final stretch. This chapter is necessary for both hobbyist and career pilots. Why is that? As a hobbyist, you will likely want to explore beyond the local area. You will want to venture further. For career pilots, every subsequent checkride involves cross-country flight planning, including Instrument, Commercial, and CFI.

What are the two primary navigation methods?

Pilotage and dead reckoning.

What is pilotage?

Using visual landmarks for navigation.

What is dead reckoning?

Deriving the current position, or a future position, mathematically from a planned position or the last known position using winds, sectional, timing and calculations.

What type of charts would you use for basic VFR navigation?

A sectional chart and a terminal area chart (if available).

What is an isogonic line?

A line of equal magnetic variation.

What is magnetic variation?

The angle difference between magnetic north and true north.

How do you convert true course to magnetic course?

Add or subtract magnetic variation.

What is a VOR?

VOR stands for Very High Frequency Omni Range. The VOR radiates an omni-directional signal; in other words it goes out in all directions allowing pilots to fly directly to it and intercept courses. VOR has been a key navigation aid for years.

What is an NDB?

NDB, or non-directional beacon, is a radio transmitter used for navigation, though they are becoming obsolete. Few NDBs remain operational and maintained up to FAA standards.

What is RNAV?

RNAV, or area navigation, allows flight between multiple navigation aids.

What is GPS?

GPS, or Global Positioning System, enhances navigation efficiency and accuracy in aviation. Currently 31 GPS satellites orbit the Earth at an altitude of approximately 11,000 miles providing users with accurate information on position, velocity, and time anywhere in the world and in all weather conditions

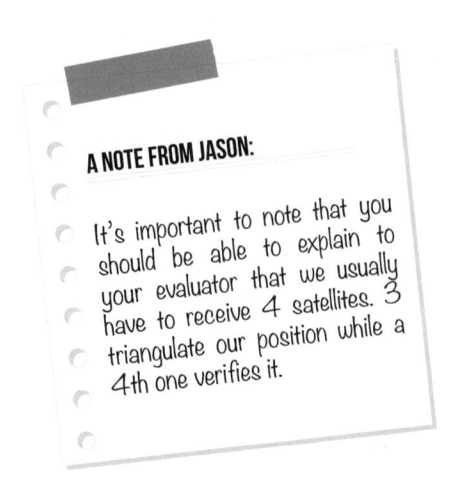

> **A NOTE FROM JASON:**
>
> It's important to note that you should be able to explain to your evaluator that we usually have to receive 4 satellites. 3 triangulate our position while a 4th one verifies it.

What are the different methods of checking a VOR for accuracy?

Ground Check

You would taxi to a designated area on the field and turn the OBS to a certain heading while on the proper frequency and note accuracy. Maximum tolerance is plus or minus 4 degrees.

Airborne Check

Select a VOR radial that lies along the centerline of a VOR airway. Select a prominent ground point more than 20 NM from the VOR facility. Maneuver airplane around the point at a lower altitude noting the bearing. Maximum tolerance is plus or minus 6 degrees.

Dual Check

If the airplane has two VORs, you can tune them to the same VOR facility with a TO indication. Note the indicated bearings to the station. Maximum tolerance is plus or minus 4 degrees.

What is DME?

DME stands for distance measuring equipment. When tuned to a VOR frequency that also has DME, it gives you distance information from that facility. Keep in mind that this is in slant range. Meaning if you're right overtop of the VOR facility at 6,000 feet it will show you 1.2 miles away from the VOR because of your altitude.

What are the Four C's of your lost procedures?

- *Confess* – Admit to yourself that you are lost.
- *Communicate* – Inform others of your situation. Contact local air traffic controllers and ask if they can help find you.
- *Climb* – Altitude is your friend, climb so you can see better.
- *Conserve* – You don't know how long it will take for you to regain your bearings. Conserve your fuel.

How do you activate a VFR flight plan?

You can activate your VFR flight plan several ways.

On the ground at an uncontrolled airport, you can call 1-800-WX-BRIEF to activate it. If you are operating out of a controlled airport, ATC can assist you.

If you are already flying, you can call a Flight Service Station over the radio. You can find the proper frequency on your sectional chart on top of the VOR communications box. Some VOR frequencies include an "R" at the end like 122.1R. What does the "R" mean? The R means ATC receives your voice on 122.1 which means you must transmit on 122.1. You will hear FSS over the VOR frequency. Be sure to have the volume up! In situations where there is no "R" you simply transmit and receive on that same frequency.

If you filed your VFR flight plan with LEIDOS, you will be emailed an "easy activate" link, which allows you to open the flight plan yourself when ready. Some EFB's like Foreflight give pilots the ability to open and close VFR flight plans directly through the app.

What is a DVFR Flight Plan?

Any time flying across an international border you need to file what is known as a Defense VFR flight plan or be on an IFR flight plan. Because of security, this type of plan is required to identify who you are and your intentions as you fly into another country. If you choose to fly through an ADIZ under VFR, then you will need to choose VFR on the ICAO flight plan and then choose "D" for DVFR under flight type.

What is CRM?

CRM stands for Crew Resource Management. How well are you working with your crew members? CRM helps pilots reduce error and conduct safe and efficient operations. For example, if you're flying with another pilot in a busy Bravo airspace you could say, "Hey, you work the radios and I'll focus on flying the aircraft."

CONCLUSION

We at MzeroA hope that you enjoyed using the Pass Your Private Pilot Checkride book! We enjoyed compiling this list of most often asked checkride questions to help you prepare for your big day. By studying hard and continually working on your piloting skills, no doubt that you will find success!

MzeroA offers support in your learning with our Online Ground Schools, Bootcamps, free videos, multitude of training books and more. The MzeroA Nation Facebook group is a community of pilots always supporting one another, please join if you have not yet done so. It is also a great source of information. We are always here and ready to support your piloting needs. You can always reach out to support@MzeroA.com with any questions.

Keep up the great work in your pursuit of aviation mastery. Thank you for being part of the MzeroA community. We hope you continue to stay with MzeroA for all of your training needs. We love to read your success stories! Please share when you have passed your checkride and can call yourself a Private Pilot!

Don't forget that a good pilot is always learning!

Many Blessings,

Jason Schappert

NOTES

NOTES

NOTES

NOTES

NOTES

Made in the USA
Columbia, SC
03 March 2025